SEASON OF GRACE

Finding Freedom from
Panic Attacks, Fear, and Anxiety

by Russ Pond

Dedication

To Angela,
Thanks for walking with me, side by side,
through this journey of grace and freedom.

To those teachers and ministers
who taught me about the finished work of Christ
and the freedom it brings,
Thank you! And keep spreading the Word.

Table of Contents

INTRODUCTION

My Personal Battle with Fear and Panic Attacks

As I've grown in my faith over the years, my perspective has changed when it comes to freedom. Most of my experience with fear has been spent coping, covering, and numbing the pain. It has only been in the past year or so that I've actually begun pursuing true freedom—the kind of freedom where coping, covering, and numbing are no longer needed.

My story starts decades ago, when I was a child lying in bed at night experiencing this overwhelming sense of fear and dread. I would lie in bed trying to go to sleep, my mind wandering anxiously from thought to thought. Then, one night, I had this thought about dying and being trapped in a lifeless body unable to move, staring into darkness for all eternity. This terrifying thought would trigger waves of panic in me. I would often jump out of bed and run to my mom, screaming at the top of my lungs. The fear was incredibly intense.

In the 70s, there was no name for this "condition" that we now refer to as panic attacks. I spent countless hours in the doctor's office trying to describe this indescribable feeling. They would often diagnose me with stress, prescribe some tranquilizers, and send me on my way. I was just sixteen years old when they started medicating me for this unknown "stress" condition.

I pushed through high school with sporadic outbreaks of panic. I would be sitting in class like any other day, and all of sudden my body would go numb, and my heart would start racing. Fear would hit me hard, but I wouldn't move. I didn't want anyone to know what was going on. It was incredibly terrifying.

When I started college, I discovered a form of self-medication—alcohol. It was cheap, effective, and readily available. The problem is that alcohol created these incredibly anxious, morning-after experiences. One hung over morning, while driving to San Antonio for a job, I was hit with the most terrifying panic attack I had ever experienced. My mind was racing uncontrollably, and I thought I was losing my mind. I kept thinking to myself that I was going crazy. *This is what going insane must feel like.*

After a few terrifying hours of complete panic, I was able to get back home and try to sort through all those confusing thoughts. Still, I had no answer for these crippling, terrifying episodes of fear. A few years later, when the attacks started to increase, I met with a psychiatrist in Austin. After one visit, he pulled out this big, black book and had me read a section titled "Chronic Panic and Anxiety Disorder." I read through that description and was totally shocked. All of sudden, this "condition" had a name. Not only that, there were others struggling with this disorder. I sensed a bit of relief that day.

I moved to Dallas after graduating college to go to work full-time. Even though I now had a name for this condition, the anxiety and panic attacks continued. In 1991, at my wits' end, I started looking for a church. I was very curious about faith, and if anyone could help me find healing, I knew God could. I found a church in November of 1991. Shortly after attending a few times, the pastor began sharing his own experience with panic attacks. It was amazing to find someone who had experienced what I had experienced, and he was willing to work with me.

Over the years, the attacks would come and go. There were seasons of good and seasons of bad. However, in 2000, I decided to get off all medication and focus on fitness and nutrition. That kicked off an amazing season of peace in my life.

The year of 2000 was also the start of a new mindset for me in this battle against fear. I decided not to give into fear anymore. If fear said, *don't go there*, I would go there. If fear said, *you shouldn't do that*, I would do that. With God's strength, I faced every fear. In addition, even if I were afraid, I would do it with the fear. It was an amazing season of victory after victory. Soon, the panic attacks stopped. It was incredible!

In September of 2010, however, something odd happened. The fear and panic came back with a vengeance. Out of nowhere, one weekend I was hit with wave after wave of panic. I wasn't out of shape or eating poorly. Quite the opposite—I had been training for my first half Ironman triathlon. I was in the best shape of my life. Something else was going on, but even now, I can't pinpoint what triggered it.

It was also that year that I began this incredible quest for true freedom. I wanted a deep, soul-cleansing, stronghold-breaking freedom. So, I started reading freedom books like *Think Differently, Live Differently* by Bob Hamp; *Free Yourself, Be Yourself* by Alan D. Wright; and *Escaping the Matrix* and *Seeing is Believing* by Greg Boyd and Al Larson. Books like these and freedom ministry videos (http://j.mp/SoG-videos) were incredibly life changing.

I'm still growing and experiencing incredible depths of freedom to this day. I haven't experienced a panic attack since that terrifying weekend in 2010. I'm still hit with the occasional "sense of fear" and "dumps of adrenaline," but no full-blown panic attacks. I've also come to recognize just how much stress plays a role in panic attacks and fear.

My understanding of freedom continues to grow each and every day. If you're struggling with fear, anxiety, and panic attacks, know this: God is fighting for you, and he wants to help you experience complete freedom. In addition, he has given us freedom through Christ. I encourage you to learn about God's plan for freedom in your life.

Prayer: *Father, open up my heart to your plan for freedom. Show me more about how to get completely free from the fear, anxiety, and panic attacks.*

PART I

"Rather than define freedom as the absence of bad behavior, or the expulsion of demonic forces, we believe the Bible tells us that freedom is the not the absence of something—it is the presence of Someone. Certainly some things get in the way, but removing them does not equal freedom. Freedom is when you engage the presence of God and become the person you are created and redeemed to be."[i]

— Bob Hamp

The Foundation

I want to start by laying some groundwork for freedom—what it is and what it isn't.

There are times we get caught up in something that binds us, hinders us, and keeps us from walking the abundant life. Therefore, we pray and plead with God to take it away, but freedom seems so elusive sometimes. We pray harder, we fast, we start bargaining with God, yet the fear is still there. The panic still hits.

When I was at this place in my life, I just assumed that God wanted me to go through this "wilderness of fear" to help me grow in him. I rationalized that panic attacks were from God to make me a better Christian. On the other hand, maybe it was that I needed more faith, more righteousness. If I could just do well enough, or strive harder to be better, then surely, God would set me free. However, I realize now that that kind of thinking is not biblical.

Let me start with God's heart toward you. In John 10:10, Jesus tells us very clearly what the devil's motivations are and what God's motivations are.

> *The thief does not come except to steal, and to kill, and to destroy. I have come that they may have life, and that they may have it more abundantly.* (John 10:10)

My theology is pretty simple. God is good. The devil is bad. I believe with all of my heart that God has great plans for you (see Jeremiah 29:11-14), that God is for you, not against you (see Romans 8:31). Jesus made it clear that he has come to give us not just life, but abundant life. In addition, he makes it very clear that the devil comes to steal, kill, and destroy. Think about fear, panic, and anxiety—does it steal, kill, and destroy, or does it sound like the abundant life?

I believe freedom is available for each and every one of

you. Whatever is holding you back—fear, panic, anxiety, depression, whatever—God has made a way for you to experience abundant life through Christ.

As you read through this, it's very important for you to understand God's heart toward you. He is on your side. He wants you to walk in peace, not in bondage. He has great plans for you, plans to give you an abundant life in Christ. Moreover, *"if the Son sets you free, you are free indeed"* (John 8:36).

In this book, we're going to dig into some of God's truths about freedom. I hope to tear down some of the lies that are keeping you in bondage. Truth will set you free. I can promise you that through Christ, because he himself said, *"You shall know the Truth, and the Truth will set you free"* (John 8:32).

Are you ready for freedom?

Prayer: *Father, prepare my heart to receive your Truth. I want to know your freedom-empowering Truth. Make it clear to me that your heart toward me is good, and that you're on my side.*

Focus

When struggling with an issue in your life, it's hard not to focus on the problem. In fact, the most common response is to "try harder" or "learn more" or "fight, fight, fight!" Therefore, we pour energy, time, and resources into overcoming the problem. We believe that focusing on the problem will help us overcome it.

- *If I could just stop eating so much, I could finally lose some weight.*

- *I hate it when I yell at my kids. I wish I wasn't so angry all the time.*

- *I will not be like my mom. I will not!*

Here's the problem with that thinking: **What you focus on organizes your life**.

If you focus on fear, then fear organizes your life. If you focus on overcoming anger, then anger organizes your life. Whatever your focus on will organize your decisions, your thinking patterns, and your way of life.

Do you remember the Chinese finger trap toy? As a kid, I played with these all the time. You put your finger in one side and someone puts their finger in the other side. As you each try to pull your finger out, the "trap" tightens making it harder to escape. Your strength makes the problem worse.

The same is true about focusing on our problems—the more we focus on them, the tighter the grip and the harder it is to escape.

So, what's the answer? **Change your focus.**

In Matthew 6, Jesus talks quite a bit about the struggles we face here on earth and encourages us not to worry. His solution was not to focus on the problems. His solution was to

> ...*seek first the kingdom of God and His righteousness.* (Matthew 6:33)

Jesus encourages us not to focus on our problems but to focus on God, because when we focus on the Kingdom of God, then the Kingdom of God organizes our lives.

So, how do you focus on the Kingdom of God? Here's what Paul told the Philippians:

> *Fix your thoughts on what is true and honorable and right. Think about things that are pure and lovely and admirable. Think about things that are excellent and worthy of praise.* (Philippians 4:8)

As it says in Romans 12:2, we must change the way we think and renew our mind. For freedom to happen, we must change our focus and seek first the Kingdom of God and his righteousness. When we do, then freedom will organize our life!

Prayer: *Father, give me a Kingdom focus. Help me to cast all my cares upon you for you care for me (1 Peter 5:7).*

Author's Note: *Thanks to Bob Hamp (http://BobHamp.com) for teaching these incredible freedom principles. Check out his book,* Think Differently, Live Differently.

The Right Source

When the phone rang, the young sixteen-year-old boy answered. It was his aunt. Her car had a flat tire, and she couldn't change it herself. She needed his help.

The young boy hopped into his small, American car and headed her way. When he arrived, he was eager and ready to change her tire, but she didn't have a lug wrench for her German-made car. *No problem.* The young boy grabbed the lug wrench out of his American car, not realizing that the US-made lug wrench used inches and the German-made wrench used millimeters. *That's okay*, he thought. *It still fits.*

He used the jack to lift the car up and then placed the wrench on the first lug nut. *Feels snug.* So, with all his strength, he twisted the lug wrench. He felt it moving, but it slipped a few times. That was okay; he was strong. He continued to push the wrench round and round, not realizing he was stripping the lug nuts.

Not sure what was happening, he tried the next lug nut. Same thing. Then the next one and the next one. When he was done, all but one of the lug nuts were ground down to a finely polished surface. Nothing would grab them now. He thought he was fixing the problem, but now the problem was worse.[ii]

This story illustrates a profound truth in my experience

with panic attacks. There are many "tools" out there today that promise freedom. In fact, I tried almost all of them. However, now that I am free, I have realized that most of these tools actually did more damage than good. Like this lug wrench story, the wrong tool even in the right hands can create more problems than it solves.

So then, what is the right tool for freedom?

Humanity has two key problems:

1) We are born into this world disconnected from the Source of true life.

2) Because of that, we have connected with ourselves as our own source.[iii]

Think about it: when struggling with crippling fear, anxiety, depression, and panic attacks, do you find yourself with these thoughts?

- *If I just had enough courage, I could beat this thing.*
- *If I could find the right book, tape, or doctor, then I could get free.*
- *If I could just find the right medication, then I would have peace.*
- *If I just prayed the right prayer, then God would answer.*
- *If I just had more willpower, I would be able to overcome this.*
- *If I fight hard enough, I can win this battle.*

The problem with these types of thoughts is that we think we are the source of our freedom, but we're not. We can't fix ourselves. It's like trying to arm wrestle with yourself—even if you win, you lose.

Have you heard this phrase: "God helps those who help themselves"? Guess what? It's not in the Bible. It's not scriptural. It should say, "God helps those who cannot help themselves." On the other hand, let me say it this way:

> *When we were utterly helpless, Christ came at just the right time and died for us sinners.* (Romans 5:6)

> *Trust in the LORD with all your heart; do not depend on your own understanding.* (Proverbs 3:5)

> *Whoever clings to this life will lose it, and whoever loses this life will save it.* (Luke 17:33)

The harder you work at fixing your own problems, the harder you turn that wrongly-sized lug wrench, the more damage you do.

Believe that God is working in you with his divine tools to transform you. Mick Mooney describes it this way: "Our job is to believe, God's job is to transform. Our job is to believe, God's job is to produce the good fruit in our lives by his Spirit."[iv]

I encourage you today to stop using the wrong tool. Set it down. Give it to God.

> *Cast all your anxiety on him because he cares for you.* (1 Peter 5:7)

Connect with your True Source of freedom. Let him whisper his love over you, because he wants you free more than you do. So, let him take you there.

Prayer: *Father, I've been working so hard for so long with the wrong tool. I give up. I'm tired of doing more damage than good. I lay down my tools, my efforts, even my strength, and I put all of my trust in you, for you alone are my true Source of peace and freedom.*

Is it Physical, Mental, or Spiritual? Yes.

When it comes to anxiety and panic attacks, I'm often asked if it's a physical experience, a mental struggle, or a spiritual battle. In my own experience, and what I've heard from others, it's rooted in all three.

Think about water for a moment. It can exist in three distinct states: liquid (water), vapor (steam), and solid (ice). Like water, our being consists of three distinct elements—physical, mental, and spiritual. Paul closed out his first letter to the Thessalonians with this encouragement,

> *May the God of peace himself sanctify you entirely; and may your **spirit and soul and body** be preserved complete, without blame at the coming of our Lord Jesus Christ.* (1 Thessalonians 5:23, emphasis mine)

That is my prayer over you as well, that God would help you find freedom in your spirit and soul and body.

I hear many stories from those struggling, and very few pursue healing in all three areas. Often, people will pursue a bodily solution (like medication and exercise), but neglect the mental and spiritual aspects. Others may combine body and soul (like exercise and counseling), but neglect the spiritual. Even faithful believers may focus primarily on the spiritual side of freedom (prayer and deliverance) but neglect the physical and mental aspects.

True freedom comes when you address all three parts.

The Body

Panic attacks are a very physical experience. Your body responds with increased adrenaline, rapid heartbeat, shallow breathing, and increased blood pressure. It's getting ready to run or fight. Blood is pumped to your arms for fighting and legs for running. (Ever notice your hands tingling or getting cold?) Acid is released in your stomach to quickly digest food for energy. (Ever get butterflies in your stomach?) Your body is responding to a threat, either real or imagined.

There are certain triggers that can escalate that fight or flight mode, like caffeine or sugar. In addition, there are physical things you can do to reduce the anxiety, like exercise or medication. Early in my struggles, I found some peace with medication, but today I'm medication-free by focusing on diet and exercise to help me release that excessive adrenaline. (There may be medical triggers causing the anxiety and panic attacks. While it's very rare, you should talk to you doctor.)

The Soul

The soul is your mind, that part of you that makes choices. The soul is where your memories live and your emotions are experienced. It's an incredibly complex system of thoughts, ideas, choices, and perspectives.

It's also where anxiety and panic attacks are triggered. Just like the body can trigger those terrifying feelings, so can your soul. Maybe it's a traumatic memory or a painful wound; the soul can initiate those experiences with fear.

When I was in college and the "episodes of fear" were rampant in my life, I made an appointment with a counselor who began sharing with me information about a term I had never heard before: "panic attacks." A few years later, I began meeting regularly with a pastor who had experienced the same thing and was now free. He began to teach me how to renew my mind, my thoughts, and my choices (Romans 12:2). However, he didn't stop there. He began to teach me about...

The Spirit

Understanding the spiritual side of panic attacks changed everything for me. I believe it's what gave me the edge to find true, complete freedom. Sadly, I believe it's where most people fall short. The more I began to understand the truth, the more freedom I began to experience.

> *You will know the truth, and the truth shall set you free.* (Romans 8:32)

Regarding the spiritual side of fear and panic attacks, here are some key topics that opened the doors to freedom in my life:

1) Grace

Understanding the finished work of Christ and all he has done for us has revolutionized my relationship with God. (My messages on grace are included in this book. They can be found in Part IV.)

2) Authority

Even today, I don't completely understand all of the authority that we truly have as believers. God has given us amazing authority here on the earth (Luke 10:19), and I believe the enemy's greatest strategy is to keep us blind to our authority.

If we truly knew how big and powerful we are in Christ, and just how small and powerless the enemy is, it would change everything.

3) Freedom

Combining all that I learned about the spiritual side of freedom, I chronicled my journey; the results of that journaling can be found in Part I of this book.

Prayer: *Father, help me understand the importance of all three areas — body, soul and spirit. Teach me to put all my trust in you, and help me to know the truth so that I can walk in true freedom.*

What Causes a Panic Attack?

Panic attacks are caused by a variety of issues. It's a multifaceted condition that varies from person to person. Everyone's situation is unique, but there are patterns and common experiences that seem to trigger those unwanted adrenaline bursts.

Before understanding the cause of panic attacks, we need to understand what exactly a panic attack is.

What Is a Panic Attack?

When panic strikes, it may feel like the entire world is crashing in around you. Your heart is pounding and your mind is racing. You become hyper-focused on your surroundings, and the desire to run or fight is very strong.

While it may feel foreign and terrifying, this experience is a very natural experience. God wired every creature with this built-in defense mechanism, which is triggered by adrenaline. When faced with a dangerous situation, your body and mind respond with this fight or flight condition.

Imagine walking through the woods, hiking by yourself. You push your way through the thick woods and reach a clearing. There in front of you, drinking in the stream, is a giant bear. He hasn't seen you yet, but your situation just became very dangerous.

At this point, your body responds. Adrenaline is immediately pumped into your system. Your heart rate spikes. Your blood pressure increases. Your breathing gets shallow. Your body starts pushing blood to your hands for fighting and to your legs for running. Your eyes dart around, efficiently searching for an escape. You are now in fight or flight mode.

In this situation, the danger is obvious—a bear. However, for those who experience a panic attack in the comfort of their homes or at a grocery store, this is terrifying because there is no bear. Your body is acting like there's a serious threat to your life, but as you look around, there's no threat.

Traumatic Events Can Trigger Panic Attacks

For decades now, I've talked with thousands of people who have experienced panic attacks, and it's very common to hear stories of traumatic events. Trauma is a very common trigger for panic attacks. In a traumatic situation, your body goes into this fight or flight mode, and, like a computer, the event is programmed into your mind, along with those sensations that come from the adrenaline rush.

Later in life, you may be sitting at home reading a book and, all of sudden, that same rush of adrenaline sweeps over you, and those feelings of panic come rushing in, but there's no traumatic event happening at that moment. It's hard to know what triggers those memories, but it's a common experience among panic sufferers. Most panic memories are rooted in lies and agreements.

Lies and Agreements

"If you're struggling with something, it's not because of what you are going through—it's what you believed while you were going through it."[v] This is so true with panic attacks. They are often rooted in lies and agreements. Let me give you an example.

One day after school, you're headed home on your bike, and you're about to cross the street. Smash! You see a car accident right in front of you. The loud crash and the shock of the event immediately send you into fight or flight mode. Maybe someone is hurt, and maybe you see people bleeding or crying. It's a very traumatic situation.

Our enemy hates us, and he will often use traumatic situations in our lives to implant lies. While your body is experiencing this normal adrenaline-raised situation, he whispers, *You can't trust God to protect you. He could take your life in a second.* If you're not grounded in God's truth or surrounded by wise counsel, you will agree with that lie. It all seems to make sense on the surface. Then that traumatic event is programmed into your mind while being associated with the lie that you can't trust God.

If the lie continues to grow deeper into your soul, it will become harder for you to function in everyday situations. You could be driving your car to the store, and then a thought comes into your mind: *You could be in a wreck.* Then the lie kicks in: *And you can't trust God.* Those programmed memories rise up, and your body for some reason goes into fight or flight mode. Panic hits. There's no real danger, but the lie has been programmed by the enemy to create fear and panic.

Finding Freedom

Jesus came to set you free (John 8:32). He can help you re-program your mind to believe in the truth. Not only does he have the desire to do it, he has the power to do it. The more we surrender to his power and his work in our lives, the clearer our thinking can become, and peace will follow.

> *There must be a spiritual renewal of your thoughts and attitudes.* (Ephesians 4:23)

Prayer: *Father, help me re-program my mind by the power of the Holy Spirit. Renew my thoughts and attitudes that I may experience your peace.*

What Is Stress?

When it comes to fear, panic attacks, and anxiety, stress can be a key trigger. What is stress, and how does it affect us?

Here's one definition of stress: "*a state of mental or emotional strain or tension resulting from adverse or very demanding circumstances.*"[vi]

Stress has many forms and can be caused by a variety of things. Trying to pin down the causes of stress may be difficult because it varies from person to person. What may be stressful for me may not be stressful for you. It's a very personal experience but often has very common results.

Stress and Panic

I have found in my own life that stress is one of the key triggers for anxiety and panic attacks.

For the past few years, I have not struggled with panic attacks. Nevertheless, today, when things get stressed in my life because of work or other issues, I experience what I call "adrenaline zaps." Small, little dumps of adrenaline surge into my body that temporarily get my heart racing. In the past, it would often have resulted in panic, but today I recognize those "zaps" and immediately take steps to keep the panic from hitting.

Recognize Stress

When those "zaps" hit me, I first deal with that excess adrenaline to make sure it doesn't turn into full-blown panic. I don't stop there. I start to think through the past few days and weeks. What is going on that is putting my body and mind under stress? Is it a project deadline? Too much caffeine? Am I worrying about something that's out of my control? What am I doing to trigger this "zap"?

Almost always, I am able to pinpoint the stress trigger and deal with it accordingly. Most times, it's a work project that demands twelve to fourteen-hour workdays and much less sleep. I find in those times, that I have to slow down, rest, and find healthy ways to release that adrenaline, like exercise.

Deal with Stress

The first thing you have to do is recognize what is causing the increased stress levels. Once you have done that, the next step is to deal with it.

The problem is that we have an incredibly adaptable mental state. We can easily adjust our lives and our thinking around an increased state of stress. We grow more desensitized to this increased stress level, and instead of dealing with it, we numb it with busyness, food, alcohol, and other means. I believe full-blown panic hits when our desensitized stress level reaches a point that it triggers the fight or flight mode in us and we don't know why. You need to quickly respond to stress and get to the root of it as fast as you can.

While you are working through the mental and emotional causes of stress, it's important to deal with it physically as well.

Get Some Rest

Stress is often caused by overwork and long hours on the job with few breaks and lots of pressure.

When your workday is over at 5 p.m., then don't work anymore. Turn the email off. Shut down the computer. Take time every evening to rest, recuperate, and reenergize.

Sleep is God's natural way for us to heal our bodies and minds. Try to get at least seven hours of sleep, if not more. Your body wants to sleep. It's how it heals itself. Just last week, when I was fighting some serious bronchitis, I slept fourteen hours straight, because my body was healing itself through rest. So, get some sleep.

Get Moving

For me, exercise is an amazing way to deal with stress. I need to get moving. Every day, I need to do something. Even if it's a 15-minute walk, I get moving at least once a day.

Much of our stress comes from sitting at a desk all day,

working on computers, and not moving very much. I don't believe we were created to sit still. Our body just starts to shut down after sitting for a couple hours.

The more you can get your heart rate up, the quicker you can dump that excess adrenaline that's been building up in your body. Often, I'll go run or bike for an hour at the end of a workday to burn off that excess stress and adrenaline. Exercise also releases endorphins into your body, giving you a natural relaxant.

Stress can come in many forms, but the key is to recognize it and deal with it as best you can. Stress is a very personal, unique experience. I encourage you to pray and let God show you what's causing the stress. He is faithful and wants to help you.

Prayer: *Father, show me what's causing this stress in my life. Give me the wisdom and understanding I need to deal with it.*

Food and Drink Triggers

I'd like to share some of the common dietary triggers of panic attacks.

I need to start with a disclosure that I am not a doctor, a dietician, nor nutritionist. I'm simply someone who has experienced panic attacks first hand, and I've seen certain foods and drinks trigger those rushes of adrenaline.

Caffeine

Caffeine is one of the most common triggers of anxiety and panic attacks. It increases your heart rate, raises your blood pressure, and puts your body into fight or flight mode. Too often, we seek that rush of energy that comes from a strong cup of coffee or an energy drink. We push ourselves to work harder and longer, not taking time to let our bodies and minds rest.

If you drink a lot of caffeine, it would be smart to taper off slowly and let your body adjust to the change.

Sugar

I believe sugar is another very common trigger. Most junk food today contains lots of sugar. The rise and fall in blood sugar can trigger anxiety and panic attacks. You need to avoid high-sugar snacks and find a more healthy way to boost your energy, like fruit with its natural sugar.

Alcohol

One of my worst panic attacks happened after a night of drinking in college. The morning after was horrific. My nerves were on edge, and it created the perfect environment for a mental meltdown. You should avoid alcohol. The alcohol converts to sugar, creating those spikes and falls in your blood sugar. In addition, the alcohol will leave you anxious and nervous the next day.

Starchy Foods

Starchy foods can also make your blood sugar fluctuate. Our family keeps the starchy foods—like potatoes, rice, breads, and pastas—to a minimum.

MSG

I've personally never had a bad experience because of MSG, but I've read stories about how MSG can trigger panic attacks. I typically avoid MSG in my diet.

Lactic Acid

Lactic acid occurs naturally in your body after a strenuous workout. Your body stores this lactic acid, and it crystallizes in your muscles causing the soreness.

Some people claim that lactic acid can increase the anxiousness and even cause panic attacks, but I haven't had this happen to me that I'm aware of. Certain foods and drinks have lactic acid in their ingredients. Be sure to read the labels.

Exercise

While it may seem contradictory for me to list exercise right after lactic acid, I have found exercise to be remarkably beneficial in alleviating the symptoms of anxiety, fear, panic, and stress. Your body's natural fight or flight mode automatically releases adrenaline in your system, increasing your heart rate and blood pressure. It's preparing it to run or fight. Exercise is a great, healthy, natural way to release that built up adrenaline in your system. In addition, it releases the natural endorphins in your system, creating a sense of peace and rest in your body.

I've already mentioned that exercise has been incredibly helpful to me in fighting through stress, panic, and fear; I often run and compete in various athletic races. I started doing triathlons a few years ago and my wife and I competed in a local sprint triathlon recently. After the triathlon, I felt so good, so peaceful, and so restful. I can't recommend exercise enough.

Real Freedom

Please keep in mind that learning the dietary triggers and how to avoid them is not a real solution to freedom. These are only triggers. It is absolutely essential that you find true freedom. As I've stated quite a few times before, freedom happens through Christ as he brings complete healing to your body, soul, and spirit.

Prayer: *Father, as I learn more about these sensitivities in my body, please help me along my path to true freedom in Christ.*

The Caffeine Trigger

Over the past decade, there has been a substantial increase in the consumption of caffeinated drinks. These include coffee, soda, tea, and energy drinks like Red Bull, Monster, Rockstar, and 5-Hour Energy. All of these include stimulants that can increase your heart rate and blood pressure, triggering the fight or flight condition in your body.

Without a doubt, caffeine is one of the key culprits in triggering anxiety and panic attacks. Here are four things to keep in mind about caffeine:

1) Association

Many people associate caffeine intake with anxiety, fear, and panic attacks. While there can be some physical association, it must be understood that caffeine is not the root problem for anxiety and panic attacks. Root causes are often tied to emotional wounds and traumas that need a much deeper healing than simply eliminating this stimulant.

Caffeine is just a trigger of other deeper issues that need to be addressed. True freedom comes when you find healing from inner traumas and deep-rooted lies.

2) Desensitization

People who have experienced anxiety and panic attacks are often overly sensitized to certain sensations, feelings, and emotions. The stress put on the body increases your central nervous system's sensitivity. Desensitization is essential for healing. You must find ways of reducing stress and working through those things that increase your stress levels. One of the ways you can desensitize yourself is...

3) Elimination

Since caffeine is a known trigger for anxiety and panic attacks, eliminating it from your diet can be one of the most beneficial steps in finding freedom. Removing this stimulant from your daily routine can help bring down your adrenaline and cortisol levels, making it easier for you to work through the root issues that cause anxiety and panic.

It's recommended that you do not quit caffeine cold turkey. The sudden elimination of caffeine is widely known to have certain withdrawal symptoms. Headaches are the most common symptom. If you are unsure on the best way to eliminate caffeine from your diet, then talk to your doctor.

4) Moderation

So, are those morning cups of latte bliss and mocha joy forbidden forever? For a few people, maybe, but I don't think everyone has to quit caffeine indefinitely. Once those root issues are dealt with accordingly, and the emotional triggers are gone, then most people can moderately introduce caffeine back into their daily life.

In my life, there was a season I could not drink any caffeine—no soda, no coffee, and no tea. Today, however, I enjoy a couple cups of coffee in the morning and maybe a glass of iced tea in the afternoon. I completely avoid energy drinks because most of them have stimulants and chemicals designed to get your heart racing. For me, it's just not worth it. I moderate my caffeine based on my sensitivities.

Prayer: *Father, show me if my caffeine intake is a culprit, and then give me the wisdom and strength to cut back or eliminate it.*

Medication for Anxiety and Panic Attacks

I am always hesitant to share about medication in fighting anxiety, because it has been a very sensitive issue in my own life. After receiving many emails over the years about medication, I know it's a sensitive issue for others. My goal is to simply share my own experience with medication for anxiety and panic attacks and to hopefully answer some questions you may have.

First of all, let me state that I'm not a doctor or physician. I've had no medical training, so what I share is from personal experience. Every decision I made about medication was with my doctor's guidance and blessing. I did not make any decisions or take any action regarding medication without my doctor's approval. I did, however, take control of my medication situation. So, please consult your doctor when it comes to medication.

In my high school years, before stress, panic, and anxiety were well-studied, I was prescribed my first benzodiazepine. Benzos, as they are sometimes called, are a class of medications often prescribed for anxiety, panic attacks, sleeplessness, and other conditions. Some brand name benzo medications include Valium (diazepam), Xanax (alprazolam), Klonopin (clonazepam), and Halcion (triazolam). In high school,

I would only take the medication when I was feeling anxious or struggling with sleep. Moreover, it was quite effective.

Receiving my "Chronic Panic Disorder" diagnosis in college helped. It was the first time in my life that I had a name for this condition. I actually felt some relief knowing that I wasn't alone. However, the anxiety and panic attacks continued to get worse. By the time I was out of college and working, I was taking Klonopin on a regular basis. I carried a couple pills with me at all times "just in case."

There were times I tried other medications, like SSRIs (selective serotonin reuptake inhibitors). These are antidepressants that are sometimes used to treat anxiety disorders, but I didn't like the way they made me feel. My mind was too foggy. There were other non-benzo medications for anxiety that I tried, like Buspar, but it didn't really do much for me. The benzos were the quickest acting and the most effective.

When 2000 rolled around, I was taking Klonopin almost every day, and the panic attacks were at their worst. I just couldn't understand why this medication wasn't working like it used to. Was my tolerance changing? Was my body getting used to it? Did I need a new medication? I just didn't know.

It was also an interesting time for me regarding my

spiritual walk. I was growing in the Lord, learning more about faith and God. I had so many questions like:

- Should Christians rely on medication?
- Was I sinning by taking medication?
- Did God want me to get off medication?

I had lots of questions but few answers. I asked around and the responses were varied, even extreme at times. Nevertheless, I had to find an answer soon, because the panic attacks were getting worse, and the medications were not working. I'll admit that I tried stopping the medication a few times on my own, but the panic returned violently. It was not a good idea.

I began researching benzos and long-term use and found that not all doctors agree on the effectiveness of long-term use. I knew benzos were like alcohol, in that you could become physically addicted and that a tapering system should be followed if you planned to stop taking them. I found some online forums and started talking with people who had gotten off benzos after years of use. After praying about it, I felt like God wanted me to get off this medication.

I called and made appointment with my doctor and explained to her that I wanted to taper off the medication. I explained my situation, what I had learned, and what I intended to do. She was hesitant but agreed to work with me. After a prolonged tapering program, I was off the medication in October 2000.

I'll admit it wasn't easy. Nevertheless, it's been almost thirteen years, and I haven't taken any medication for anxiety or panic attacks since then. Interestingly, panic attacks no longer control my life as they did. I believe, in some ways, the ups and downs of the benzos were actually triggering the anxiety and panic. I don't know for sure, but it's very interesting to me that things began to settle in my mind after getting off the medication. I used this new clarity of mind to get counsel, from people and from the Holy Spirit, and began dealing with some deep issues in my heart. I knew true healing would be both physical and mental.

Today, I have a much different view on medication than I did back then. I believe anxiety and panic attacks are a mental and emotional condition rooted in patterns of wrong thinking and lies. Freedom comes from changing those patterns and renewing our minds (Romans 12:2). Sometimes, we need medication to get us to a place where we can receive help. Our nervous system and adrenaline glands may be overly sensitized making it difficult to receive healing. Medication can be used temporarily to get us to a place of healing. After my experience, I don't believe long-term use of certain medications can bring true healing.

I am confident that everyone can experience healing and freedom for chronic anxiety and panic attacks.

Everyone's path to freedom is unique, but God promises to *"guide us along the best pathway for our lives"* (Psalm 32:8). If you're taking medication, be smart in how you pursue freedom. Talk to your doctor and make sure you walk in wisdom and seek counsel. Find someone you trust and let them speak into your life—maybe a pastor, an elder, or a church counselor.

Prayer: *Father, you desire to guide me along the best pathway for my life. I put my trust in you. You are my Hope. You are my Strength.*

Will These Panic Attacks Ever Go Away?

I've asked this question hundreds of times, maybe thousands of times. I've even waffled in my answer over the years. Am I destined to live with panic attacks the rest of my life or can I be free?

When I was younger and the panic attacks were frequent, I was desperate for hope. I was searching for something to alleviate that onslaught of fear and confusion. Alcohol provided temporary relief, but it always left me more anxious and panicky the next day when it wore off. Medication was helpful, but, like alcohol, the panic and fear would return after the medication was out of my system.

I spent lots of time sitting in front of counselors, psychiatrists, doctors, psychologists—anyone who could help me get free from this terrifying condition. However, for years, there was no relief. It was then that I landed at the conclusion that maybe, like diabetes or high cholesterol, I would have this "disease" for the rest of my life. I had lost hope.

Then, something happened that changed everything. I met a gentleman who had lived a life of fear and panic attacks, but now he was free. Could it be? Can you get free from fear and panic attacks?

This new information set me on a course to learn as

much as I could about freedom from fear, anxiety, and panic attacks. Here's what I learned:

Freedom Is Possible

Too often, we convince ourselves that freedom is impossible or elusive. We often let our experiences and feelings determine what's true for us. We may even start to think freedom is possible, and then hope builds, but WHAM! An attack hits, and we lose hope again.

The key for freedom is what you choose to believe. You have to believe that freedom is possible. Freedom will never come if you do not change the way you think. If you don't know where to start, then start with a prayer asking God to transform your thinking.

> *Don't copy the behavior and customs of this world, but let God transform you into a new person by changing the way you think.* (Romans 12:2)

I believe that everyone can experience freedom from anxiety, fear, and panic attacks. It is not something you have to live with the rest of your life. You can be free!

Freedom Is a Process

Most people want instant freedom, but this often leads to discouragement. We want to pray a powerful prayer to receive a heavenly zap that'll take it away, but I don't know that prayer. It has been my experience that freedom is a process. For some, it's a quick process, and for others, it's a bit longer. I also know others who have found freedom immediately upon "hearing" God reveal the truth about a lie at work in their lives.

The key is to get started. Once you believe that freedom is possible, you can start taking steps to get free.

> *Do not despise these small beginnings, for the LORD rejoices to see the work begin.* (Zechariah 4:10)

Freedom Is for Everyone

Sometimes, we convince ourselves that freedom is for others but not ourselves. Again, we often let experience and feelings dictate this lie in our lives. We want freedom, but we don't experience it, so we wrongly conclude that we'll always have this "condition." That's just not true.

It is absolutely essential for you to understand that freedom is available to you. Jesus paid an incredible price so that you can boldly approach God in your time of need.

> *Let us therefore come boldly to the throne of grace that we may obtain mercy and find grace to help in time of need.* (Hebrews 4:16)

In Christ, you have everything you need to receive freedom (Ephesians 1). Let this message plant a seed of hope in your heart. Today, I am walking in incredible freedom from fear and panic attacks, and so can you!

Prayer: *I pray that God, the source of hope, will fill me completely with joy and peace because I trust in Him. Then I will overflow with confident hope through the power of the Holy Spirit (Romans 15:13).*

PART II

How to Not Fight Fear

When it comes to overcoming fear, one of the most important tools I learned was how to not fight fear.

It's actually quite a paradox. When fear strikes, your instinct is to fight hard against the onslaught of confusing and tormenting thoughts. Your body releases adrenaline, and immediately your entire physiology changes to face a threat.

Here's the problem: There's typically no real danger or physical threat. Much of our bodily response is a direct result of our thoughts. It's a vicious cycle. First you have a thought, and then your body responds. The additional adrenaline intensifies those confusing thoughts, which releases more adrenaline releasing more confusing thoughts. It grows and quickly spins out of control. Wham! A full-blown panic attack!

Early in my search for freedom, I read a couple of excellent books on the subject. Dr. Claire Weekes wrote two books called *Hope and Help for your Nerves* and *Peace from Nervous Suffering*. There was one thing that stood out from her books that really gave me an edge in this battle with fear, and that was the concept of "floating a thought."

The concept is relatively simple to understand but a bit more difficult to apply. When a fear thought comes into your mind, don't fight it and don't resist it. Simply let it "float on past." Let it come and let your body dump the adrenaline, but don't respond to it. Don't give in. Just let it float into your mind and pass on through.

I remember my first key victory over panic attacks. I was sitting in a recliner holding my three-month-old son at my in-laws. Fear hit. My body went numb. The panic attack felt imminent. But, instead of fighting the fear, I decided to just let it come. It did, and it passed. No panic attack. It was amazing!

Here are some steps to remember when a panic thought invades your mind:

Recognize

You know that feeling well. A thought hits you and your body starts to react.

The first thing you need to do is recognize that thought. Recognize that it's a fear thought, and that it's not a real threat. Once you recognize what it is, then...

Don't Fight It; Float It

As the fear thought hits you, don't resist it. Don't fight

it. Let it come and tell yourself, *I will not resist the fear thought.*

It's like a campfire. When I was a boy scout, we would make fires by getting some small embers going. Once they were going, I would blow on them to make them burn hotter. You would think that blowing on them would make them go out. However, that's not what happens. Instead of extinguishing the embers, you are actually blowing more oxygen into the flame, feeding the fire. The same is true with fear. When you fight it, you feed it.

It's very counterintuitive to not fight the fear, because everything in your mind and body says FIGHT! What has helped me the most was learning how to...

Trust in the Lord

When Moses and the children of Israel were fleeing Egypt, Pharaoh and his army were hot on their trail. As they approached the Red Sea, there was no escape. They were trapped by the mountains on each side, the sea in front and the approaching army behind them. They were gripped with fear. Then the Lord spoke to Moses, and Moses answered the people, *"Do not be afraid. Stand still, and see the salvation of the LORD"* (Exodus 14:13a).

God said to them, "Don't fight. Just trust me. Stand still and I will rescue you."

I know firsthand how terrifying and confusing those fear thoughts can be. I know how hard it is not to fight. However, I've also seen how the Lord can rescue those who "stand still" and trust in him. He is faithful. He will not let you down!

Prayer: *Father, the next time a fear thought hits me, give me the courage to let it come and float on past me. I will not fight. I will stand still and trust you to rescue me.*

How Exercise Can Help

When stressed, your central nervous system becomes highly sensitized to the increased adrenaline levels. Our bodies were designed to respond to threats with this fight or flight response, but anxiety, fear, and chronic panic experiences keep the body at this heightened state of stress, making it difficult to shut down and relax.

A common physical response to fear and stress is the release of cortisol in our bodies. Cortisol is a hormone produced by the adrenal glands. It regulates blood pressure and the body's use of fats, carbohydrates, and proteins. Many experts refer to it as the "stress hormone," because cortisol secretion increases during stressful situations. Excessive cortisol in the system also suppresses the immune system, making it difficult to fight off diseases, viruses, and sicknesses.

Exercise is a very effective means for reducing adrenaline and cortisol levels in the body. Sadly, today's modern lifestyle doesn't produce much physical activity. Just a few generations ago, life was much more active. Our daily activities back then included working the land, farming, and hunting. In addition, transportation was not as common as it is today, so we walked everywhere.

Today, life is very different. We drive our cars to the store to shop for food. We often buy pre-made food that only requires a little preparation. During the day, we usually sit at a desk for hours and then drive back home to sit in front of our TVs. Life today is very convenient and very simple—and very sedentary. It's why so many people struggle with weight issues today.

I work from home, so it's even easier to be lazy and snack all day, so fitness has to be a part of my daily routine Today, I try to be very active, exercising almost five or six times a week. (It helps that my wife is a personal trainer.)

Here are some of the key benefits of exercise that I have experienced:

Reduces Stress

As I said earlier, exercise reduces the adrenaline levels and the cortisol in your system. Physical activity makes you less stressed. Difficult issues are easier to handle, and you are less likely to snap at others.

Produces Peace Endorphins

Exercise produces endorphins that create a sense of peace and pleasure. Sometimes, the release of these endorphins are referred to as a "runner's high." After a hard race or triathlon, these endorphins flood my body, and it's one of the most peaceful and relaxing times for me.

Helps with Sleep

I used to have problems going to sleep at night. My mind would race and I would often lie in bed for hours thinking and dwelling on various things. Once I started exercising, it was very easy to fall asleep and stay asleep. Last year, during my triathlon training, I slept so well, often getting eight and nine hours of solid sleep a night.

Improves Immune System

Another great benefit of exercise is a strong immune system. Since becoming active, my wife and I rarely get sick. We average about one or two sick days a year and it's often just a quick, 24-hour virus our son brings home from school.

Keeps the Fat Away

Everyone knows that physical fitness is essential to maintain a healthy weight and to lose those extra pounds. Doctors used to recommend physical activity three times a week, but now it's suggested that you be physically active for at least thirty minutes every day. Even walking for thirty minutes a day can be beneficial.

I would encourage you this week to think about ways to get moving and stay moving. Remember that exercise is like medication—it's good to help deal with the symptoms of anxiety, fear, and panic attacks, but you should also seek wise, biblical counseling to work through the emotional strongholds that are causing the problems.

Prayer: *Father, give me the strength to start exercising on a regular basis and help me find ways to stay active.*

How to Stop Anxious Thoughts

Our struggle with anxiety and anxious thoughts primarily happens in our minds. What we think and believe often affects what we experience physically. Let me show you.

As you read this, imagine yourself holding a lemon. Now, really try to imagine it. Look at it. Feel the texture. Smell it. Now take a knife and cut the lemon in half. The smell is stronger now. Close your eyes and imagine taking a big, juicy bite of the lemon.

Did your mouth water? Or, maybe reading this caused your mouth to pucker. If you really imagined that lemon in your mind, then, most likely, it did. I find this experiment amazing, because it proves that a thought can trigger a physical, chemical response in your body. If that's true, then surely anxious thoughts can produce chemical reactions in your body.

Here are four practical steps on how you can stop anxious thoughts:

1) Recognize

First, you need to recognize an anxious thought as simply that: a thought. It's only in your mind. In most situations, there is no real danger. Too often, we've built a pattern of dangerous thoughts in our minds that really have no danger.

If we can start by recognizing those anxious thoughts when they come, and see them simply as thoughts, then it becomes easier to stop them. It helps to write down irrational thoughts when they hit. When you have a thought that doesn't feel right or brings anxiety or confusion, write it down and take note of how it makes you feel. Keep a journal. This will help you recognize certain patterns in how you think.

2) Take Those Thoughts Captive

When an anxious thought hits you, it's essential to capture that thought immediately and think through where it's coming from. Remember, the enemy can put thoughts into your mind and make them sound like your own. Don't believe everything you think. Look at the fruit of that thought. Does it produce peace or fear? If it produces anxiety, fear, or heaviness, then don't receive it. It's not from God. Reject it as a lie and ask God to give you peaceful thoughts.

For though we live in the world, we do not wage war as the world does. The weapons we fight with are not the weapons of the world. On the contrary, they have divine power to demolish strongholds. We demolish arguments and every pretension that sets itself up against the knowledge of God, and we take captive every thought to make it obedient to Christ. (2 Corinthians 10:3-5)

The Bible says we must renew our minds and stop conforming to the patterns of this world (Romans 12:2). This world—with its horror movies, fear-inducing reality shows, depressing news broadcasts, and unstable economy—will not produce peace. Quite the opposite. My family and I no longer watch the news on TV. We don't watch horror movies or television shows that would produce anxious thoughts.

3) Find a Healthy Release

I have found exercise to be an extremely helpful release of adrenaline. At the end of the day, when anxiety levels are raised, I often go for a run or a bike ride. The exertion is very good for ridding your body of the excessive adrenaline. If exercise is not an option, then spend time in prayer, meditation, and reading Scripture. Flood your mind with God's truth and his promises of peace over you.

4) Get to the Root

It's like a splinter in your finger. You can clean it, numb it, and cover it, but if you never remove the splinter— the very cause of the pain—it'll never heal. It'll just get more painful. In the same way, until you properly deal with the "splinter" in your mind and thoughts, you'll never really find true freedom from anxious thoughts and worry.

As I mentioned earlier, freedom pastor Alan Smith

explains, *"If I'm struggling, it's not because of what I've been through. It's because of what I came to believe when I went through it. God heals me, not by changing my past, but by revealing truth and displacing lies."*

This is so true! We all have lies and wounds deep within our souls that affect how we perceive the world around us. That's why it's imperative that we *"know the truth so that the truth will set us free"* (John 8:32).

If your church does not have a freedom ministry, then I encourage you to start reading and studying all that Christ has done for you. There are some great books available. Also, check out our church's Freedom Ministry foundation videos (http://j.mp/SoG-videos). They are wonderful! In addition, you can watch them online free.

Prayer: *Father, help me recognize the anxious thoughts when they hit, take them captive, release them and then get to the root so that I may find complete freedom in Jesus.*

How to Stop a Panic Attack

When fear strikes and your body and mind move into this fight or flight mode, it can be very difficult to stop the cycle of panic. Your mind becomes a huge magnet—the closer the fear comes, the harder it is to resist.

For anyone who has experienced a full-blown panic attack or anxiety attack, it can be quite terrifying. The confusion and terror make it difficult to think clearly. Stopping the attack seems impossible while it's happening. The key to stopping a panic attack is to plan ahead and know how to respond before it happens.

Below are some steps I've taken that have been very helpful in stopping an attack:

Recognize

When panic hits, you immediately go into autopilot mode and start reacting to fear. However, you need to realize that it's just an attack. It's your body doing what it's designed to do—it's responding to a threat. The problem is that you don't know where or what the threat is, so your mind races and adrenaline is released into your body, causing the situation to spin out of control.

The first thing you need to do is recognize what is going on. Tell yourself, *This is just my body going into fight or flight mode. There is no real danger.* Recognize what's happening and remind yourself, *This has not killed me in the past, and it's not going to kill me now.* Your body is lying to you, and you need to call the bluff.

Panic can often sneak up on you before you know it and set things into motion before you have time to stop it. By recognizing those feelings, thoughts, and sensations, you can spot the precursors to panic, giving you a heads up. Then, you can move carefully and strategically into the next few steps...

Don't Fight It

Earlier, we covered the "floating a thought" method introduced by Dr. Claire Weekes. When panic hits, remember that when you fight those feelings, you are actually feeding your body more adrenaline, and you don't want that! Just let those fear thoughts "float on past."

I have found that if I can avoid fighting those feelings and let them sweep over me, that cycle of fear is broken immediately, and there's no panic. It's hard, however, to let those feelings rush in without resisting. They are terrifying. But that's why I...

Breathe Slowly

In almost every case of panic or anxiety attacks, breathing moves from a normal, slow rhythmic state to a shallow, rapid state. As your body prepares for danger, it's trying to get more oxygen into your bloodstream for the extra energy it needs to face the threat. The increase in oxygen releases more adrenaline, which you don't want.

Doctors have proven that simply by hyperventilating, you can trigger panic. The opposite is true, that by controlling and slowing your breathing, you can stop panic. It's essential to get your breathing under control. Studies have shown that by slowing your breathing, you can stop panic immediately.

Here's what I do. I start a four-by-four breathing pattern. Breathe in for four seconds, hold it for four seconds, breathe out for four seconds, and hold it out for four seconds. Repeat. Breathe deeply with your abdomen, watching your stomach move in and out.

It may be hard at first because your body is not used to slower breathing in a panic state, but I have found repeatedly that this step is very powerful in stopping panic.

Pray

Prayer is powerful! I believe God responds before we even finish praying the prayer. There are numerous examples of this in the Bible. When panic hits, call out to God for strength, wisdom, and clarity of mind to break the cycle of fear. There were numerous times that prayer alone carried me through those terrifying situations.

> The LORD says, "I will rescue those who love me.
> I will protect those who trust in my name. When
> they call on me, I will answer; I will be with them
> in trouble. I will rescue them and honor them."
> (Psalms 91:14, 15)

Faith has been essential for me in breaking the cycle of fear and panic. The more I learn to trust God, the more I can resist the urge to fight those feelings.

These are some verses in Scripture I often remember when panic strikes:

> I can do all things through Christ who
> strengthens me. (Philippians 4:13)

> God has said, "Never will I leave you; never will I
> forsake you." (Hebrews 13:5)

> Trust in the Lord with all your heart, and lean
> not on your own understanding. (Proverbs 3:5)

Call Someone

There were times when I would call someone to help talk me through the panic. While it was good in that moment to help break the cycle, you have to be very careful with this step. When you call someone in the midst of panic, and it successfully stops the attack, you can start to rely on that person for peace. That's dangerous, because you can develop an unhealthy dependency on that person or the act of calling someone. If you need to call someone, do it rarely, and don't rely on it.

I have found these steps to be incredibly helpful over the years, but please understand that these techniques are temporary. They are only coping methods that can help you through a panic situation. Complete freedom happens when you find out what is triggering these attacks, and then work through the pain, the wounds, and the patterns of thinking that cause you to experience this. Once you find freedom, the panic attacks and fear will go away. You won't need these coping techniques anymore!

Start meeting regularly with a counselor who can walk you through the pain.

These steps have helped me break the cycle of panic attacks. Today, panic no longer has a grip on me. There are a few, rare occasions where I get hit with "zaps of adrenaline," but the cycle is broken quickly, and the panic never spins out of control. As you learn these steps and trust in God, I am confident that you too can stop the cycle of panic attacks.

Prayer: *Father, give me the strength and clarity of mind to stop the panic and find freedom from what is causing this. Help me learn these steps before any panic strikes so that I can break this cycle and stop the panic attacks.*

Breaking Free from Panic Attacks

When I first become a Christian, I was still struggling with fear and panic attacks. In fact, I expected God to instantly step in and deliver me from all the fears. After all, *"God has not given us a spirit of fear, but of love, power and a sound mind"* (2 Timothy 1:7).

Nevertheless, freedom seemed so elusive.

I quickly came to the conclusion that God had given me this "thorn in the flesh" to build my character, to teach me how to depend on him. It was my "cross to bear." Now, twenty years later (and twenty years wiser), I no longer believe those conclusions. God does not give us things like fear and panic attacks to teach us something or to build our character. Yes, that can be a result of the experience, but God is not the author of confusion (1 Corinthians 14:33).

"What about Romans 8:28, that God works together all things for our good?" Yes, I believe that! I believe God can take the struggles and bad situations in our lives and use them for good, but that doesn't mean he causes them to happen. He simply knows how to turn them in our favor—to build our character and to teach us how to depend on him.

Like I've said before, my theology is very simple. God is good. The devil is bad. Jesus explains it this way:

The thief does not come except to steal, and to kill, and to destroy. I have come that they may have life, and that they may have it more abundantly. (John 10:10)

If panic attacks, fear, anxiety, and depression are taking things away from you—like joy, peace, sleep, and abundant life—then the devil is at work. He's the source of your problems, not God.

I fully believe that God is for me, not against me. His desire for me (and for you) is peace and freedom. God wants you completely free more than you do. He's working hard on your behalf to help you find freedom.

You may ask, "So, how can I find this freedom?"

It starts with agreement. You must agree with God that he wants you to live a life of peace and freedom. He is on your side. He is for you. He is waging war against the enemy of your soul—the devil. God is fighting for you.

Next, you must break those wrong agreements with the enemy. If you have settled in your heart that God is the source of your fear and panic, then you must disagree with that. Remember, the fruit of the Spirit is *"love, joy, peace, patience, kindness, goodness, faithfulness, gentleness, and self-control"* (Galatians 5:22-23). Do you see fear, anxiety, torment, sleeplessness, dread, terror, or depression listed there? No. That's because God is for you, not against you!

Take a long, hard look at what you have believed about your struggles with fear. If you have believed this condition is from God, then you are believing a lie. The enemy is trying to confuse you. He wants you to believe this is from God so that you will remain trapped in fear the rest of your life. Don't believe it. God is on your side! Who the Son sets free is free indeed! (John 8:36).

Prayer: *Father, please help me know that you are for me, not against me. Show me how to agree with you and your plans, and how to break all of the wrong agreements I have made that are keeping me trapped in this situation.*

PART III

Wired to Malfunction

The counselor looked me right in the eye, pointed at me, and said, "You are a Ferrari!"

I smiled. He definitely had my attention, but I was curious what he meant.

"You are this incredibly efficient machine, built for speed and performance." I started to smile. Then he really got my attention.

"But you're malfunctioning. Someone has put bad gasoline into you, and you are sputtering along. You can't operate at the full capacity that you were designed to operate."

Something rang true in his words. I knew that the anxiety, fear, and panic were not supposed to be part of my life. I was wired for joy and peace. I was created for so much more, things like "*love, joy, peace, patience, kindness, goodness, gentleness and self-control*" (Galatians 5:22, 23).

He went on to explain that God's desire is for us to live an abundant life (John 10:10), and to live that life dependent upon him (John 15:5), not upon ourselves. If we're not living the way God created us to live, then we will malfunction and experience things like anxiety, fear, insecurity, frustration, anger—those things that we know aren't right within us.

God loves us so much that he wired us to malfunction—not to cause us pain or misery, but to help us get back on track to the abundant life he created us for. If my incredibly fast and efficient Ferrari is sputtering along at 10 miles per hour, then I'm going to work hard to find out what's wrong. I'll take it to a specialist who can find the cause of the problem and fix it. In the same way, if you're experiencing fear, anxiety, or panic attacks, ask God to be your Specialist. He sent his Holy Spirit to counsel you and to guide you into all truth.

> *When the Father sends the Counselor as my representative—and by the Counselor I mean the Holy Spirit—he will teach you everything and will remind you of everything I myself have told you. I am leaving you with a gift—peace of mind and heart. And the peace I give isn't like the peace the world gives. So don't be troubled or afraid.* (John 14:26, 27)

Ask the Holy Spirit to show you if there are any lies at work in your life. Lies are always "bad gasoline." Believing lies is the key reason why we malfunction and start experiencing things like anxiety, panic, and fear. When we believe a lie about ourselves or about God, our minds and bodies respond to the lie as if it were true. When we think a lie is true, it sets in motion a series of painful, emotional experiences. We start to malfunction.

We must recognize the lies and start taking steps to tear them down. We must replace those lies with God's truth. When we do that, we shall know the truth and the truth will set us free (John 8:32).

Prayer: *Father, I know that you've created me for so much more. I am a Ferrari, but something is malfunctioning in me. Help me tear down those lies that are keeping me from living the abundant life. Help me to know the truth.*

Finding the Cause

If you're experiencing something in your life that is causing pain or discomfort—fear, anxiety, depression, panic attacks, anger, emotional pain, or maybe some addiction—then somewhere in your life, there is most likely a deep-rooted lie at work in your thoughts and choices.

That's a bold statement, but listen carefully to what Jesus said,

> *You shall know the truth, and the truth will set you free.* (John 8:32)

If knowing the truth sets you free, then believing a lie will keep you from being free.

Before going deeper, let me lay some scriptural groundwork:

- All truth comes from Christ. He is the Truth (John 14:6), and he speaks truth in our lives to set us free (John 8:32) so that we can live life more abundantly (John 10:10).

- All lies come from the devil. He is the father of lies (John 8:44), and he uses them to "steal, kill and destroy" (John 10:10).

Anything in your life that is keeping you from living life more abundantly is based on a lie that you believed, and the enemy is the one who spoke it to you.

Recently, my son and I saw *Inception*. (Spoiler ahead, so don't read the rest of this paragraph if you want to see the movie.) The premise of the movie is about a small band of dream thieves who travel into people's dreams to implant ideas while the person is sleeping. The main character is hired to go into this man's dream, not to steal information, but to plant an idea at a deep, sub-conscious level, because if the man believes that thought to be true, he'll change the way he lives and start making choices based on that idea.

This is exactly how the enemy works. If he can subtly get us to agree that something is true when it's not, then we'll make choices and base our actions on that lie. The result is pain, both emotional and physical. Thankfully, pain is God's way of telling you that something's amiss, something needs fixing. Pain is often God's way of letting you know there's a lie at work in your life.

> *Faith comes by hearing, and hearing by the word of God.* (Romans 10:17)

To start getting to the root of the lie, we must start "hearing" the truth. We must replace that lie with God's truth, but we can only know that the lie is a lie when we understand more of God's truth. Through prayer, Bible reading, Godly counsel, learning, and just "listening" to God, you can start tearing down the lies. Sometimes, it can happen quickly. Other times, it takes time to retrain your mind.

I encourage each of you to pray a very simple prayer and then "listen" carefully for the Holy Spirit to speak to you:

Prayer: *Holy Spirit, please reveal to me any lie at work in my life that is keeping me from knowing the Truth that will set me free.*

Recognize the Lies

The Lord used a wayward prophet's donkey to speak and get his attention. Recently, the Lord used some fictitious underwater sea creatures to get mine.

We've laid some spiritual groundwork to better understand that deep-rooted lies are the seed of the pain and fears you face. To recap, Jesus said,

> *You shall know the truth, and the truth will set you free.* (John 8:32)

Cornel Marais explains it this way, "If the truth has to set you free, it means you are being held prisoner by a lie. If you're being held prisoner, it means that an area of your mind has not been renewed."[vii]

We've got to renew our minds to recognize the lies and understand the truths. As you begin to dig deeper, you may ask yourself: *When did I agree with a lie? I would not have done that. Why would I agree with a lie? It sure seemed like the truth.*

Our primary battle occurs in our thought life. What we believe to be true about God, others, and ourselves, shapes our interpretation of life's events and the meaning we assign to them. Our thought life is the battleground. Do your thoughts obey and represent Christ in you and his finished work on the Cross?

*For though we walk in the flesh, we are not
waging war according to the flesh. For the
weapons of our warfare are not of the flesh but
have divine power to destroy strongholds. We
destroy arguments and every lofty opinion raised
against the knowledge of God, and **take every
thought captive** to obey Christ.* (2 Corinthians
10:3-5, emphasis mine)

When I take a thought captive to obey, I must recognize
the source from which it originated. From whom was it
born? Was it truth that originated with Jesus and what
he is speaking to me through his Spirit, or is it a lie from
the father of lies?

Thoughts are always drifting through our minds at any
given moment. Thoughts that come from a bad
experience are often used by the enemy to create lies in
our minds. Whether it's a subtle word spoken in anger
or maybe something more traumatic, truths and lies
will swirl around in our thoughts, seeking a place to
land, giving you the opportunity to interpret God,
others, yourself, and the meaning of that experience. It
is at those times that you are most vulnerable to agree
with the lies.

As I was learning to recognize the lies in my life, I
discovered an example of the battle for my mind while
watching an absorbent, yellow, and porous, sea sponge
named SpongeBob SquarePants.

In the video, the "truths" that SpongeBob and his friend Patrick are passing to each other are shown in "bubbles" that are meant for each other. Just as the Spirit speaks to me, telling me my Father's purposes and plans for me as shown through Jesus, so these two friends were speaking to each other. However, there is another voice. Squidward, who intercepts the friendly messages and substitutes his "lies" to change SpongeBob's and Patrick's perception of each other and even their friendship.

I too have another voice and source of thoughts that drift through my mind. He has lies to bind me into traps and painful ways of thinking about God, others, and myself. Moreover, these lies always sound like my own voice.

I want to encourage you to start asking the Holy Spirit to reveal the sources of your thoughts. Jesus told us that the Spirit would guide us into all truth (John 16:13). Ask him to show you if there are any lies at work in your life that may be causing you fear or pain. Ask him to show you any ungodly agreements you may have made.

Prayer: *Holy Spirit, teach me to recognize the lies that present themselves as truth. Give me understanding of the source of the thoughts that drift through my mind. Give me strength in the battle for my mind to bring my thoughts to obedience by agreeing with truth and not lies.*

Finding the Truth

The enemy can keep us from freedom through his lies. I believe that his only weapon against us is his ability to lie to us and get us to agree with him. For example, I believe sickness can only come upon us when we believe a lie. Our bodies are amazing. God created them very carefully and very specifically to respond to thoughts, ideas, and beliefs. Your thoughts can create a physical effect in your body.

Remember the lemon for a second. Imagine holding it again, looking at it, and smelling it. It does not have that strong of a smell. Now imagine taking a knife and cutting the lemon in two. The smell is a bit stronger. Now, take a big, juicy bite of the lemon.

Did your mouth water again, thinking about it? Probably. Or maybe reading this caused your mouth to pucker again? Where's the lemon? There is none. Just me putting a thought into your mind was enough to produce a biological, chemical reaction in your body. Your chemical balance was physically affected by a thought I put in your mind. If that's true, how much more can the enemy affect your body's biological response?

Thoughts, ideas, beliefs, emotions, feelings, and painful memories can produce a physical response. Panic attacks and anxiety are a physical response.

I heard a story from Bob Hamp, our church's freedom pastor, which really illustrates how truth can effectively set us free, even within our physical bodies. He was once counseling a woman who was mad at men for the way they treated her, and she was angry with women for not protecting her. She was pretty messed up. Besides the addictions and outbursts of anger that plagued her life, she had become genderless. She hated men, and she thought women were weak, so she sided with neither. She wore genderless clothes, avoided contact with people, and considered herself neither female nor male.

Over time, Bob helped her through the anger issues and the addiction issues and was making great progress. One day, he looked at her and said, "God made you woman." Her face contorted and the anger started to rise up. "Women are weak!" she spouted back. Bob pointed to a few women she knew who were strong, who were good leaders, and who made good decisions. She started to soften a bit. He went on to explain to her that, physically, God created her as a woman. Her body was that of a woman, whether she believed it or not. The truth started to sink in.

A few days after that session, Bob received a call from the woman. "I need your help, Bob." He was excited to help.

"What do you need?" he asked.

After a bit of awkward silence, the woman said, "Well, I just started my cycle."

Bob wasn't sure what to do. "And, uhh, how can I help?" This woman was 36 years old. Surely, she knew what to do. Her response shocked him.

"I've never had a period before. This is my first. I don't know what to do." The truth was starting to affect her physically. Her body was starting to line up with how God created it.[viii]

What an amazing illustration of how a lie can make our bodies not function the way God created them to function. In addition, it shows how the truth can set us free and help our physical bodies line up with how God created us to live life.

We've spent a lot of time talking about truth and lies, their source, and how they affect us. I want to encourage you to dig really deep, seeking God and asking him to show you any lies that you have believed.

Prayer: *Father, you are the Source of all truth. Help me find the source of the lies that are at work in my thinking patterns, my memories, my thoughts, and my decisions. Show me through Scripture, through dreams, through counsel, through your still, small voice what lies are at work in me. Then, through the power of Christ, help me tear down those lies and replace them with truth.*

Hearing God's Voice

There has been one thing that has consistently moved me down the path of freedom: hearing God. The more I tune into his tender voice, the more freedom I experience in every area of my life.

The Word gives us a very good reason for wanting to hear God's voice:

> *I listen carefully to what God the LORD is saying, for **he speaks peace** to his people, his faithful ones.* (Psalms 85:8, emphasis mine)

God is constantly speaking peace over you. For anyone struggling with fear, anxiety, panic attacks or depression, God is speaking peace over you right this very moment. Like an old radio, we must learn to tune into God's peace-speaking voice.

Here's another wonderful Scripture that should encourage us to want to hear God's voice:

> *If you need wisdom—if you want to know what God wants you to do—**ask him, and he will gladly tell you**. He will not resent your asking. But when you ask him, be sure that you really expect him to answer, for a doubtful mind is as unsettled as a wave of the sea that is driven and tossed by the wind.* (James 1:5-6, emphasis mine)

In every area of our lives, we need wisdom. Wisdom is

what gives us a God-directed strategy that will never fail. Never. In addition, wisdom is essential if we want to find freedom from fear. James encourages us to simply ask for it, and when we ask, God will "gladly" tell us.

Throughout the Bible, there are numerous verses and examples about hearing God. It's God's desire to speak to us and guide us. He speaks to us in the Psalms.

I will guide you along the best pathway for your life. I will advise you and watch over you.
(Psalms 32:8)

As a father myself, I know how important it is for me to consistently communicate to my son, for him to hear my voice. How can I expect to educate him, train him, discipline him, and guide him if he can't hear me?

What's it like to hear God's voice?

One of the most confusing things about hearing God's voice is that we don't "hear" anything. It's not an audible voice, as if talking to a friend on the phone. God is Spirit (John 4:24), so he most often uses a spiritual voice to speak to us.

So, what does a spiritual voice sound like? When I hear God, it comes in the form of my own thoughts, but different from my personal thoughts. I often exercise my spiritual ears in my morning journaling time. Using my computer to journal, I type black letters when I'm praying, asking, or just talking to God. Moreover, when I want to hear God, I change the font color to red or *italics* and just start writing what comes to my mind. What often happens is that I end up writing something that I know is not birthed out of my own thoughts. God has spoken.

Let me give you an example from a journal entry a few days ago:

> Father, when I start to feel this anxiousness arise in me, can you let me know how I should respond, or what I should do? I don't want to just numb it, or cover it, or distract it. I want to know what you think I should do when it comes over me.

> *Seek first the Kingdom, and all the things you need will be given you. Son, don't seek peace, seek Christ because he is Peace. Don't seek freedom, seek the Lord because he is Truth and the Truth sets you free.*

I try to journal like this daily, because I want to hear God daily, and I know he wants to speak to me. By doing this on a regular basis, I can tune my spiritual ears more and more to hear God's voice.

Here's the most wonderful part—He desires to speak to all of you. I'm not special. I simply believe that Christ is now our High Priest (Hebrews 2-4) and that he has made a way for us to come boldly to God's throne of grace in our time of need (Hebrews 4:16). Moreover, if you are in Christ, you can hear God, too.

When you start listening for God's voice, you must remember that he will never speak anything contrary to what he has revealed in his Word. The Bible should be your filter when hearing God. In my journal example above, the first and last sentences God spoke to me were Scripture. God always uses Scripture as a foundation for his voice. Always. That's why it's helpful to have a regular Bible reading plan. The more you know the Bible, the easier it is to know his voice.

Prayer: *Father, help me hear your voice more clearly. Teach me how to discern your voice in the midst of a busy world. Help me be still so that I can know you are God.*

Who is That Speaking?

When it comes to "spiritual hearing," a common question arises: *Who said that?*

I have struggled with the discernment of whether or not I was hearing God speak to me. When I do hear what I think is God whispering to me, I wonder if that was him. Or was it just me? Or was it the accuser, Satan? As we will learn about later, the voice of God is not typically audible—heard through our natural sense of hearing. He speaks to us in our spirits, which comes to us more in our own inner voice—or thoughts. Even a knowing or an intuition.

One day, Jesus explained to a gathering of people why he would do the things he did, such as healing a man on the Sabbath. This was considered a violation of the Law of God by the religious leaders of the day and could not be done. However, Jesus replied to them,

> *By myself I can do nothing; I judge only as I hear, and my judgment is just, for I seek not to please myself but him who sent me.* (John 5:30)

According to that scripture, what could Jesus do? Nothing! By himself, he could do nothing! Jesus only did as he heard. He listened and then judged those thoughts he heard.

Judge, judged, judgment—it can be a loaded word. Here

it simply means "to distinguish properly." Jesus properly distinguished the source of the thought. It was not himself. The voice was from either his Father or his accuser. He always judged righteously because he only wanted to please the One who sent him, his Father.

Sure, Jesus could hear the accuser in his thoughts, but he knew the voice of his Father, and he would not agree with any thoughts from the enemy. He only agreed with his Father. Jesus never agreed with the accuser. He never allowed the accuser into his heart; therefore, the accuser never had any hold over Jesus (John 14:30). Think about when Jesus was tempted in the wilderness (Matthew 4). In the wilderness, he heard the tempting thoughts of the accuser but countered with Truth from Scripture.

This should be exciting news for every believer! Jesus is the firstborn of many, the new creation in a fallen world. We are born again into this new creation as Jesus was. We are to live as he did here on earth. I am born again into the new creation that Jesus provided for us.

Therefore, I am to judge the thoughts that present themselves in my mind. I need to judge the source or originator of every thought that comes in. We are told in Scripture to take every thought captive to the obedience of Christ (2 Corinthians 10:5).

God only speaks truth, because he is truth.

> *He is the Rock, His work is perfect; for all his ways are justice, A God of truth and without injustice; Righteous and upright is he.*
> (Deuteronomy 32:4)

Satan, the accuser, only speaks lies.

> *[Satan] was a murderer from the beginning. He has always hated the truth, because there is no truth in him. When he lies, it is consistent with his character; for he is a liar and the father of lies.*
> (John 8:44b)

I was created to judge (properly distinguish) the thoughts presented before me. The thoughts I agree with begin to fill the storehouse of my heart. If the agreements are good and truthful, then my heart is filled with goodness and truth. I will then speak and act similarly. If the agreements are evil and untruthful, then my heart is filled with lies and deception, and I will speak and act similarly.

The more I know my Father, the more I know Truth; I can begin to distinguish my Father's thoughts, which are truth. Let me give you an example. Take a few quiet moments to see if you can hear this thought in your mind: *Child, I love you.*

Now, who said that?

Satan cannot speak this statement to me, because he is a liar and this statement is truth. I cannot speak or make up that statement because I only know I am loved by God because he revealed it. Therefore, it was God, for he alone is truth and can speak that truth to me. Once I know I hear his voice—"I love you" —I can begin to tune into other things he is speaking to me, and tune out the things that don't matter.

As I was learning to hear my Father's voice, a minister once said to me, "The only thing that matters is what God, my Father, has to say about every second of my life." It is vital that I know his voice, agree with him, and allow his truth to rule and reign in my life.

Prayer: *Father, help me know you so I may know your truth. I choose to agree with your thoughts for me and about me. I want to have ears for you and you alone.*

Seeing with Spiritual Eyes

Each of us experiences this world through our five senses—touch, taste, smell, sound, and sight. It's how God created us. However, he didn't stop there. He also created us with spiritual eyes and spiritual ears to see and hear things that are spiritually discerned.

One of the phrases that Jesus used often was

He who has ears, let them hear. (Matthew 11:15)

Was he saying that lots of people back then didn't ears? No. He was calling upon people to open up their spiritual ears, to hear what God was saying to them.

In my own battle with fear, I often find myself focusing on life through my natural senses and very little on my spiritual senses. Too often, I let what I feel or what I see determine what I believe. However, that's backwards. I need to let what I believe determine how I feel and even what I see, spiritually.

Let me explain it this way: there is a difference between *facts* and *truth*. Facts are what you experience naturally, with your five senses. Truth happens at a deeper level, at a spiritual level. Very often, truth must be seen with spiritual eyes. Let me give you some examples:

The *fact* is I feel depressed. I feel too weak to do anything because I feel so weighed down. The *truth* is I can do all things through Christ who gives me strength

(Philippians 4:13).

The *fact* is I feel so alone in this struggle with fear and panic. The *truth* is you are never alone. God promises, *"I will never leave you nor forsake you"* (Hebrews 13:5).

The *fact* is you just lost your job, and you have bills to pay. The *truth* is if you seek first the Kingdom of God, he'll provide for all your needs (Matthew 6:33).

The *fact* is you feel powerless to overcome these struggles in your life. You feel powerless to pray, to read the Bible, to spend time with God. The *truth* is the same power that raised Jesus from the dead lives inside of you (Ephesians 1:19-20).

The challenge for us is that from birth we've been taught to only trust in our natural senses. We've been programmed to only interpret life through what we experience here on earth, but Jesus has come to reprogram us. Romans 12:2 tells us to not be conformed (molded) by this world, but be transformed by the renewing of our minds. We must reprogram our thinking to focus on truth so that it can supersede the facts of our situation.

When we focus on facts, we focus on the carnal (natural) things of this world. However, when we focus on truth, we focus on the spiritual things of God. There is peace when we are spiritually minded, but there is fear, depression, and anxiety when we are naturally minded. This scripture makes this clear:

> *For to be carnally minded is death, but to be spiritually minded is life and peace.* (Romans 8:6)

If you want life and peace, then you must become spiritually minded.

Yes, we live in this natural world, and every day we are faced with natural things. It's how life happens. Jesus did not come to take away our natural life—he came to give us life more abundantly (John 10:10), by empowering us to interpret things differently, spiritually. We must have spiritual eyes to see truth, and when we do, the natural things in our lives will become less important. That's why Paul, in the book of Colossians, encourages you to

> *Set your mind on things above, not on things on the earth.* (Colossians 3:2)

In Matthew 14, Jesus was with a multitude of people who came to him for prayer and healing. It was getting late, and his disciples asked Jesus to send the multitude away so they could go eat. Jesus said, "You give them something to eat," but all they had were five loaves and two fish. Jesus asked them to bring him the little food they had and then asked all the people to sit down. Now listen carefully to what Jesus did.

He took the five loaves and the two fish, and
looking up to heaven, *he blessed and broke and*
gave the loaves to the disciples; and the disciples
gave to the multitudes. So they all ate and were
filled, and they took up twelve baskets full of the
fragments that remained. (Matthew 14:19-20,
emphasis mine)

This phrase "looking up to heaven" is very interesting.
The original Greek word for "looking up" is *"anablepo."*
It literally means "recovery of sight." It was used when
Jesus healed blind people, and they "recovered their
sight," or they *"anablepo."* When Jesus was with this
multitude of people, the *fact* was there was not enough
food to feed them. The disciples could see that.
However, Jesus saw the *truth*. He *"anablepo* to heaven"
or he "recovered his heavenly sight." It was then that he
blessed the food and the miracle took place.

My prayer is that God will help me *"anablepo* to
heaven," that he will help me recover my heavenly sight,
so that I may have spiritual eyes to see the truth, and
not just the facts.

Prayer: *Father, open my spiritual eyes to see the truth of*
who you are and who I am in Christ.

A Spiritual War

In your struggle with fear and anxiety, you must realize that it's a spiritual battle. Yes, you walk in the flesh and live your life in this world, but the battle, the conflict, the struggle happens in the spiritual world. Additionally, to fight this battle, you cannot rely on worldly weapons. You need to think spiritually and use the spiritual weapons God has given you.

What are your spiritual weapons?

> *Therefore take up the whole armor of God, that you may be able to withstand in the evil day, and having done all, to stand. Stand therefore, having girded your waist with truth, having put on the breastplate of righteousness, and having shod your feet with the preparation of the gospel of peace; above all, taking the shield of faith with which you will be able to quench all the fiery darts of the wicked one. And take the helmet of salvation, and the sword of the Spirit, which is the word of God.* (Ephesians 6:13-17)

These are the weapons of our warfare:

- The belt of truth (to conquer the enemy's lies)
- The breastplate of righteousness (for you are righteous in Christ)
- The shoes of peace (to walk in peace)

- The shield of faith (to extinguish the fiery darts of the enemy's lies)
- The helmet of salvation (for in Christ, you are bound for heaven)
- The sword of the Spirit, the Word of God (hearing God's voice)

These are spiritual weapons. They are how you wage war against the enemy. We battle with truth, righteousness, peace, faith, salvation, and the Word of God. So, how do we fight with these spiritual weapons?

> *For though we walk in the flesh, we do not war according to the flesh, for the weapons of our warfare are not of the flesh, but divinely powerful for the destruction of fortresses. We are destroying speculations and every lofty thing raised up against the knowledge of God, and we are taking every thought captive to the obedience of Christ.* (2 Corinthians 10:3-5)

These weapons are "divinely powerful" to tear down the enemy's strongholds and fortresses that cause fear and anxiety. Specifically, we can use our spiritual weapons to "destroy speculations" and "every lofty thing" that comes against God's truth.

First, we must destroy "speculations." These are the arguments that the enemy puts into our minds to confuse us. Remember, he's the father of lies. He may try to put thoughts into your mind like, *I better not leave my house. It could be dangerous.* We respond, *But, I've been outside before, and I was fine.* The enemy responds again, *But things are different now. The world is not safe.* Back and forth, this war of thoughts is waged and lies are used to confuse and create fear in us. Don't even go there.

Secondly, we must destroy "lofty things." These are those thoughts that try to torment us. *I wonder if this is cancer. Cancer killed my uncle, and now it's coming for me.* Or how about this one: *I must be going crazy. This is what crazy must feel like. I'll probably end up in an insane asylum.* These are lofty thoughts that come against the knowledge of God, that come against truth.

We must use our spiritual weapons to battle these thoughts. We cannot give place to the enemy. We must resist the devil, and he will flee from us (James 4:7). The enemy's goal is to get your focus off God, and onto yourself and this world. If he can divide your thoughts like that, then fear, anxiety, and panic will follow. We must focus our thoughts on God and use our spiritual weapons to resist the enemy. This is God's promise when we focus our minds upon him:

> *You will keep in perfect peace all who trust in you, whose thoughts are fixed on you!* (Isaiah 26:3)

God promises you "perfect peace" when you fix your thoughts upon him.

Prayer: *Father, teach me how to use these spiritual weapons to resist the enemy, and help me to fix my thoughts upon you so that I may experience perfect peace.*

What You Already Have in Christ

When Paul was writing to Philemon, he opened his letter with a very interesting message. He said, "*I pray that you may be active in sharing your faith, so that **you will have a full understanding of every good thing we have in Christ***" (Philemon 1:6, emphasis mine).

I believe God wants us to have a full understanding of every good thing we have in Christ. What do we already have in Christ? What is ours today? I think too many believers simply pray a prayer of salvation in order to get to heaven but then stop there. What else is there? How is God involved in my life here on earth?

I've been learning that there is so much more available to us today here on earth, not just in heaven. We have so much available to us right now, but we don't know about it. We don't realize that we have access to these incredible Kingdom resources that can help us in every area of our lives.

Let me start with this. "Repent, for the Kingdom of God is at hand." When you read this, what do you think it means? Most churches today teach that we need to repent (or feel bad) for our sins, that God is going to arrive and punish sinners. So, watch out! Judgment is coming.

This is not what John the Baptist and Jesus meant when

they said,

> *Repent, for the Kingdom of God is at hand.*
> (Matthew 3:2, 4:17)

First, repentance is changing the way you think, not feeling bad for your mistakes. I cover this in more detail in Real Repentance, so I don't want to spend too much time on this. However, know this—repentance is changing your perspective, changing your worldly view into God's heavenly view. Jesus and John were instructing us to stop looking at life with our physical eyes and to open up our spiritual eyes.

Secondly, we are to repent for "the Kingdom of God is at hand." What is this "Kingdom of God"? In God's Kingdom, what would you expect life to be like? Peace, joy, love? Yes, and much more. Think about the fruit of the Spirit

> *The fruit of the Spirit is love, joy, peace, patience, kindness, goodness, faithfulness, gentleness, self-control.* (Galatians 5:22-23)

In God's Kingdom, there are all these attributes available to us. Do you long for peace? Joy? Self-control? It's available in God's Kingdom.

Finally, when can we get the Kingdom of God? Jesus said the Kingdom of God is "at hand." That phrase "at hand" does not mean far off or in the future. It means here and now. "At hand" is a phrase to indicate that it's right here, within distance of my hand. As I'm holding something in my hand, that's how close it is.

So, when Jesus said, "Repent, for the Kingdom of God is at hand," he was telling us to change the way we think about life, because love, joy, peace, patience, kindness, goodness, faithfulness, gentleness, and self-control are available to us right now. You have immediate access to these godly resources. The Kingdom of God is here with us today. Every believer has immediate access to the Kingdom of God right now.

Take a few moments to read the following promises that are available to you:

I am accepted...

- I am God's child. (John 1:12)

- As a disciple, I am a friend of Jesus Christ. (John 15:15)

- I have been justified. (Romans 5:1)

- I am united with the Lord, and I am one with Him in spirit. (1 Corinthians 6:17)

- I have been bought with a price and I belong to God. (1 Corinthians 6:19-20)

- I am a member of Christ's body. (1 Corinthians 12:27)

- I have been chosen by God and adopted as His

child. (Ephesians 1:3-8)

- I have been redeemed and forgiven of all my sins. (Colossians 1:13-14)

- I am complete in Christ. (Colossians 2:9-10)

- I have direct access to the throne of grace through Jesus Christ. (Hebrews 4:14-16)

I am secure...

- I am free from condemnation. (Romans 8:1-2)

- I am assured that God works for my good in all circumstances. (Romans 8:28)

- I am free from any condemnation brought against me and I cannot be separated from the love of God. (Romans 8:31-39)

- I have been established, anointed, and sealed by God. (2 Corinthians 1:21-22)

- I am hidden with Christ in God. (Colossians 3:1-4)

- I am confident that God will complete the good work he started in me. (Philippians 1:6)

- I am a citizen of heaven. (Philippians 3:20)

- I have not been given a spirit of fear but of power, love, and sound mind. (2 Timothy 1:7)

- I am born of God, and the evil one cannot touch me. (1 John 5:18)

I am significant...

- I am a branch of Jesus Christ, the true vine, and a channel of his life. (John 15:5)

- I have been chosen and appointed to bear fruit. (John 15:16)

- I am God's temple. (1 Corinthians 3:16)

- I am a minister of reconciliation for God. (2 Corinthians 5:17-21)

- I am seated with Jesus Christ in the heavenly realm. (Ephesians 2:6)

- I am God's workmanship. (Ephesians 2:10)

- I may approach God with freedom and confidence. (Ephesians 3:12)

- I can do all things through Christ, who strengthens me. (Philippians 4:13)[ix]

I would encourage you to read these promises constantly. Meditate on them. Let God speak to you and show you who you are in Christ.

And, if necessary, repent. Change the way you think.

Prayer: *Father, give me a new perspective on who I am in Christ.*

Having Hope

The day-to-day struggles of fear, anxiety, and panic attacks can really take a toll on your soul. Things can feel so dark and discouraging. What can you do?

I want to encourage you that there is hope. Hope is the one thing that gave me strength in the darkest of times. You need to know that there is hope in Christ.

Let me share some promises with you that will encourage you and give you hope.

God is faithful! He will complete the work he has started in you.

> *I am sure that God, who began the good work within you, will continue his work until it is finally finished on that day when Christ Jesus comes back again.* (Philippians 1:6)

May you overflow with hope through the power of the Holy Spirit.

> *I pray that God, who gives you hope, will keep you happy and full of peace as you believe in him. May you overflow with hope through the power of the Holy Spirit.* (Romans 15:13)

Strength and courage come to those who hope in God.

So be strong and take courage, all you who put your hope in the LORD! (Psalms 31:24)

God has great plans for you, and those plans include hope.

"For I know the plans I have for you," says the LORD. "They are plans for good and not for disaster, to give you a future and a hope." (Jeremiah 29:11)

When you lose hope, you can turn your thoughts toward God.

When I had lost all hope, I turned my thoughts once more to the LORD. And my earnest prayer went out to you in your holy Temple. (Jonah 2:7)

There is great hope in the Lord! You can put your trust in him, and he will pour out incredible hope into your soul.

Don't try to figure everything out. Simply put your trust in God, and don't lean on your own understanding (Proverbs 3:5). When you do, he will empower you and give you strength to stand against these attacks of the enemy.

Be encouraged! God is on your side!

Prayer: *Father, fill me with a new hope and new confidence that you are with me at all times, and that I can have freedom from fear, panic attacks, and anxiety.*

The Power of Your Words

You may not realize it, but your words hold incredible power, both positively and negatively. Everything we say aloud has the ability to influence our lives and the lives around us. God designed this world so that our words activate the supernatural.

> *Death and life are in the power of the tongue, and those who love it will eat its fruit.* (Proverbs 18:21)

We must be very careful about what we say and how we say it. It's easy to put voice to our feelings and thoughts, but are those thoughts *"captive to the obedience of Christ"* (1 Corinthians 10:5)? If our thoughts are godly, then we should speak those words of life. But, if our thoughts are birthed out of our own souls or from the enemy, then we cannot give those thoughts a voice. We must guard our mouths and avoid speaking anything that does not produce life in us and in those around us.

James compares our tongues to the rudder on a ship (v. 3:6). This rudder, though it be very small, guides and directs this giant vessel. There is tremendous power that pushes the ship through the water, but it's the rudder that guides the ship and tells it where to go. So it is with our tongues—our entire lives is guided and directed by our tongues.

I read a story about a businessman who had partnered with someone who was less than honest, and things started to go south in their business. The businessman knew his partner was being dishonest with him, but there was no proof. The businessman would come home at the end of the day and say to his wife, "This partner of mine is evil and corrupt. He's going to end up in jail and take us with him." His wife warned him about his words. She explained to him that our words are powerful, but he shrugged it off.

Day after day, he would come home and speak negatively about this partner and the business situation, and his wife would warn him. After a few months with no change in the situation, the businessman was praying, and God showed him that his words were negative and causing more problems, just as his wife had said. Immediately, God began to bless his partner, bless his family, bless his children, and bless him with success and peace. Within a week, the businessman got a call from his partner, "We need to talk. I haven't been honest with you, and I just need to make this right with you."

This story illustrates how negative words can restrict and bind the work of God in our lives and open us to attacks from the enemy. It also demonstrates how positive, godly words can release God to do amazing and wonderful things in our lives.

Assuredly, I say to you, whatever you bind on earth will be bound in heaven, and whatever you loose on earth will be loosed in heaven. (Matthew 18:18)

If you've spoken negative words over yourself or over others, don't be condemned. Jesus did not come into this world to make you feel bad (John 3:17). He came to give you life and life more abundantly (John 10:10). I would encourage you to talk to God about your words. Tell him how you've spoken out when you shouldn't have. Ask him for strength to speak words of life and words of encouragement. Then, start speaking words of life, love, hope, and peace.

A few weeks ago, I was praying and talking to God about the power of words, and God gave me a declaration to speak out loud in the mornings, and I want to share that declaration with you.

I declare in the name of Jesus Christ that:

- I am a child of God, and I have a Kingdom inheritance, today.
- I am seated with Christ in the heavenly places.
- I am free from all fear, all anxiety, all panic, all confusion.
- I am free from all sickness, all disease, all injuries, all illness, all infirmities.
- I am healed through the name of Jesus Christ,

whom I serve.
- I am at peace in my body, in my soul, in my spirit.
- I am a citizen of heaven.
- I am the head and not the tail. I am victorious.
- I am prosperous, in my soul, in my finances, in all that I have.

Each declaration is based on a promise from God in Scripture. As I speak these promises out loud, I do so slowly and methodically, making sure my heart agrees with the words that are spoken. In addition, I listen for God's agreement over these promises.

I encourage you to listen to the words you speak. Are they words of life, or words of death? Ask God to help you speak good words, godly words, words of life!

Prayer: *Father, help me guard my mouth against any negative words, and help me to speak only words of life!*

Learning to Surrender

For those struggling with anxiety and panic attacks, it often feels like we have to carry the weight, fight the good fight, and be strong. While all that may sound good, even biblical, I believe it's one of the key reasons why we can't get free. We believe we have to do all of the work.

Does any of this sound familiar?

- *If I am just strong enough, I can beat this.*
- *If I try harder, I can overcome this fear.*
- *If I can find the right book (doctor, website, resource), then I can beat this.*
- *If I just have the willpower, I can be free.*

The problem with these statements is that the burden for freedom is upon you. In fact, believing it's up to you may be the very reason you can't get free. Let me explain.

Who Does the Covering?

In the Garden of Eden, before sin happened, Adam and Eve were naked and unashamed. There was no fear, no sadness, and no lack of purpose. Life was good. Everything they needed, God provided. He was right there, walking with them, talking with them, and being their God. He was their Source for everything. Then, it happened. They ate from the Tree of the Knowledge of

Good and Evil.

Adam and Eve's first response was to hide and cover themselves. Therefore, *"they made themselves coverings"* (Genesis 3:7).

Instead of God being their sole provider, now they felt responsible for covering themselves. They carried the weight of something that was not their responsibility. Sin does that. Sin makes you feel like you are the one responsible for making things right and getting things done.

From Where Does the Power Come?

The power to get free from fear, anxiety, and panic attacks will not come from more willpower, more knowledge, or more effort. The power to get free comes from God through Christ. As you surrender your efforts and strength to God, he will move through the power of the Holy Spirit to set you free.

> *Not by might nor by power, but by My Spirit,*
> *says the LORD of hosts.* (Zechariah 4:6b)

The power of God happens when we surrender to it. If we convince ourselves that we must be strong and do this ourselves, then God graciously steps aside and lets us try. He's a gentleman. He will not force you to do something you don't want. It has to be your choice.

How Do You Surrender?

Surrender is not easy, because we are often programmed (from our culture and from our upbringing) to believe that surrender is weak. We are taught that we must be strong, that we are in charge of our own destiny, and that we are completely responsible for our fate.

While there may be some truth in those statements, the key to surrender is learning how to let go of control. To surrender, you have to give up control to God.

Here are three ways to surrender:

1) Learn to focus on today.

Do not worry about tomorrow, for tomorrow will worry about its own things. (Matthew 6:34)

If you find yourself worrying about tomorrow, ask God to help you focus on today.

2) Don't rely on your own knowledge or understanding.

Trust in the LORD with all your heart, and lean not on your own understanding. (Proverbs 3:5)

You don't have to figure everything out. Don't lean on your own understanding. Rather, trust God.

3) Don't give into the fear.

You are a slave to whatever controls you. (2 Peter 2:19)

Don't let fear tell you what to do. I have found that facing my fears head on has been wonderful in my path to freedom.

Over the years, I have learned one very important principal when it comes to facing panic and anxiety: we must completely, absolutely surrender.

Let me give you a visual example. Before you meet Christ, you're driving down this road by yourself. You're the only one in the car. Then, you see Jesus on the side of the road. So, you pull over and ask him to join you. He climbs into the passenger seat and off you go.

While on the road, you come to know Jesus and give him your life. Then you ask, "Lord, guide me, show me where to go. I surrender." You genuinely desire to do what Jesus tells you to do. The problem is that you're still driving. When you're driving, it's up to you to decide what to obey and what not to obey. This is not surrender—this is commitment. Sure, it sounds good. "I'm a committed Christian." Nevertheless, we're not called to be committed—we are called to surrender.

I recently read a great blog article called "Why I'm Not a Committed Christian - And Why That's a Good

Thing" (http://j.mp/SoG-committed). For more information on this concept, you should take some time to read this article.

We are called to surrender. Here's what we need to do: we need to stop the car, get out, and let Jesus drive. That is absolute surrender!

> *If you try to keep your life for yourself, you will lose it. But if you give up your life for me, you will find true life.* (Matthew 16:25)

So, how do we do that?

Recently, I've been reading a book by Andrew Murray called *Absolute Surrender*. (You can read it free online here: http://j.mp/SoG-Surrender). While reading this book, I keep getting stuck in chapter one, because he so wonderfully describes the surrender process. Here are the steps he describes for absolute surrender:

God Expects Your Surrender

Think of creation. The sun, moon, stars, flowers, and trees—all are surrendered to God. Murray clarifies, "Do they not allow God to work in them just what he pleases? When God clothes the lily with its beauty, is it not yielded up, surrendered, given over to God as he works in it its beauty?" In addition, God loves us so much that he has given us the choice to surrender to him, and when we do, we can be all that he created us to be.

God Accomplishes Your Surrender

I love this! It is God who works in us and accomplishes the surrender for us. Murray writes, "God does not ask you to give the perfect surrender in your strength, or by the power of your will; God is willing to work it in you." Do we not read: *"It is God that worketh in you both to will and to do of his good pleasure"* (Philippians 2:13)?

Even if you're not sure, but you're willing to surrender, pray "Lord, make me willing."

God Accepts Your Surrender

God wonderfully accepts our surrender when we give him our lives completely. Murray said, "There is a God present who at that very moment takes possession of you. You may not feel it, you may not realize it, but God takes possession if you will trust Him." God receives you with open arms and an open heart. You don't have to be perfect to come to God. Come to him as you are, and he will accept you.

> *Let us come boldly to the throne of our gracious God. There we will receive his mercy, and we will find grace to help us when we need it.* (Hebrews 4:16)

God Maintains Your Surrender

This is also wonderful news: that it is God's duty and responsibility to maintain our surrender. It's not our burden. Murray said, "When God has begun the work of absolute surrender in you, and when God has accepted your surrender, then God holds Himself bound to care for it and to keep it." Jesus clarifies it this way,

> *Take my yoke upon you. Let me teach you,*
> *because I am humble and gentle, and you will*
> *find rest for your souls.* (Matthew 11:29)

Oh, that may find rest for our souls when we give him ourselves completely!

God Blesses When You Surrender

I believe the reason God wants us completely, absolutely surrendered to him is so that he can bless us with all the promises he has for us—promises of *"love, joy, peace, patience, kindness, goodness, faithfulness, gentleness, and self-control"* (Galatians 5:22-23). Moreover, as we surrender completely, we can then receive all the promises of God that are freely given to us as our inheritance as children of God. Murray summarizes, "This absolute surrender to God brings wonderful blessings."

Therefore, I encourage you today to stop being a **committed** Christian and start being a **surrendered** Christian. Ask God to show you what that means and how to walk it out. If you get a chance, read Andrew Murray's book.

Prayer: *Father, I know I've been driving too long, and I have not been completely surrendered to you. Lord, I am stopping the car, getting out, and letting Jesus take the wheel. I completely trust you! I surrender to you. I give you control.*

Learning to Be Still

Today's world is filled with so much "noise." Do you find yourself constantly moving, going, and running from here to there? Is something always vying for your attention?

I personally think this constant state of distraction is a specific strategy of the enemy. He knows that faith (believing) comes by *"hearing the voice of God"* (Romans 10:17). Therefore, if he can block that voice, he can successfully keep us trapped in fear, anxiety, and bondage.

That's why God tell us,

> *Be still and know that I am God.* (Psalm 46:10)

I think about Elijah on the mountain after he had been running from Queen Jezebel, who was out to kill him. He was exhausted, tired, and just wanted to die. God said, "Go stand on the mountain, and I'm going to pass by." So, Elijah went up. First, a great storm tore into the mountains and broke the rocks into pieces, but the Lord was not in the wind. And after that, there was an earthquake, but the Lord wasn't in the earthquake. Then a fire, but the Lord wasn't in the fire. Then, finally, a "still, small voice" spoke to him. It was God (1 Kings 19:10-12).

God's still, small whisper is what we need to listen for,

and we can't hear it if there are other storms in our lives like busyness, television, cell phones, Internet, meetings, video games, entertainment, etc. We must make it a daily habit to quiet our souls and our minds to "hear" and to "listen" for God to speak his whispers of love. Jesus did this often.

> *Now in the morning, having risen a long while before daylight, he went out and departed to a solitary place; and there he prayed.* (Mark 1:35)

Jesus was a busy man. He was training his disciples and constantly had people coming to him for teaching, for healing, for a touch. Yet he often got away from the crowds and distractions to quiet himself and draw from his heavenly Father.

We should do the same.

Prayer: *Father, help me clear away the many distractions in my daily life that are keeping me from hearing you. Then, help me tune in my spiritual ears to hear your voice.*

PART IV

The Love of God

When I asked the Lord what else needed to be said about finding freedom from fear, anxiety, and panic attacks, I heard that still, small whisper: "Why don't you share with them just how much I love them?"

Immediately, a Scripture came to mind,

> *There is no fear in love. But perfect love drives out fear, because fear has to do with punishment. The one who fears is not made perfect in love.* (1 John 4:18)

Our most powerful weapon against fear is the love of God. The more we learn about how much God loves us and become immersed in his unconditional love, the more freedom and peace we will experience in our lives.

The key is not just to learn about God's love for us, although that's helpful. Rather, we must experience and receive God's love. When we do that, fear will have no hold on us, and God's peace that passes all understanding will guard our hearts and minds in Christ Jesus (Philippians 4:7).

As we spend time learning about how much God loves us, I would encourage you to pray a simple prayer:

Prayer: *Father, show me just how much you really love me. Immerse me into your vast and unconditional love through Jesus Christ. Teach me and show me the depth of your love.*

Love Is His Pleasure

Too often, we view God as we view our earthly fathers. As children, before we had any thoughts of God, we looked to our earthly fathers. They were like God to us. The problem is that every earthly father falls short of modeling God. The result is that we often approach God like we approach our imperfect, earthly fathers.

I believe one of our biggest hindrances to receiving God's love is a wrong perception of his attitude towards us.

Under the Old Covenant, the people were required to perform many rituals and sacrifices to please God. These works, duties, and rituals were all part of a cleansing process that appeased God and allowed the people to come to him.

However, under the New Covenant, Jesus became our sacrifice. He performed all of the works, duties, and rituals that were required by the Law. He fulfilled the Law for us (Matthew 5:17). Under the New Covenant, all that's required to please God is to believe in Jesus.

In John 6:28, Jesus' disciples wanted to know how to please God. They asked Jesus, *"What shall we do, that we may work the works of God?"*

This is a great question! We should all ask ourselves, "Lord, what would you like me to do? What are the works that you require of me? What must I do to be pleasing to you?"

Take a moment and ask yourself these questions. Then, either written or mentally, make a list of the works you can do for God that would please him. You got 'em?

Now, let's see how Jesus answered the disciples. Jesus responded, *"This is the work of God, that you believe in Him whom he sent."*

Did you catch that? The work of God is that you believe in Christ. What pleases God is that you put your hope in Christ because he fulfilled all the Law. It's the work of Christ that makes you worthy—it's not what you do or don't do. Jesus completely pleased God, and our requirement is to simply believe that. When we fully trust that Jesus paid the full price for our sins and we receive him in our lives, then we are pleasing to God. It's not about being good enough or doing all the right things—it's about believing.

The writer of Hebrews put it this way,

> *Without faith, it's impossible to please God.*
> (Hebrews 6:11a)

When you believe in Christ, and trust in his work on the cross, then you are pleasing to God. Very pleasing! There's nothing more you can do to make yourself worthy. 1 John 5:12-13 sums it up well:

So whoever has God's Son has life; whoever does not have his Son does not have life. I write this to you who believe in the Son of God, so that you may know you have eternal life. (1 John 5:12-13)

In Christ, you are perfectly pleasing to God! He is madly, passionately in love with you. He talks about you incessantly with great pride. He rejoices over you with singing and dancing (Zephaniah 3:17). You are his favorite! You are pleasing to God!

Prayer: *Father, show me just how pleasing I am to you. Show me how much you love me and rejoice over me with singing and dancing.*

Love Is His Character

When you think about love in its purest form—unconditional, lavish, sacrificial, and unrestrained—what comes to mind? Can we even picture what perfect love looks like?

Sadly, we've been taught a wrong definition of love most of our lives. Usually it's conditional, based upon our actions or decisions. Or it's corrupted as a wounded person tries hard to share their version of love. Then there's the media, with movies and television often portraying "love" purely as a physical experience.

What would pure love look like to you?

Immediately, I think of 1 Corinthians 13, also known as the Bible's love chapter. Verses 4 and 5 provide a descriptive list of what love is:

- Love is patient
- Love is kind.
- Love does not envy.
- Love does not boast.
- Love is not proud.
- Love is not rude
- Love is not self-seeking.
- Love is not easily angered.
- Love keeps no record of wrongs.

Now that's pure love! Next time you're in a situation

where you're given an opportunity to love someone, ask yourself, *How can I be patient and kind with this person? How can I avoid being prideful, self-seeking, or rude? How can I love them sacrificially?*

It may be hard to love someone like that in our own strength. That's when we need to call upon God for his strength and wisdom, because God is love. He can show us how to love others as he loves us.

> *Dear friends, let us continue to love one another, for love comes from God. Anyone who loves is born of God and knows God. But anyone who does not love does not know God—for God is love.* (1 John 4:7, 8)

Everything God does, he does in love. Every decision he makes, every thought he has, every action he takes is rooted in love. God does nothing in your life unless it's based in love. The only language God speaks is love. When you "hear" God speak into your life, it's always words of unconditional love. It's going to sound like words from 1 Corinthians 13 above.

You may say, "Father, I really messed up this weekend, and I am so sorry for my mistakes." God says, *"I keep no record of wrongs."*

You may say, "I keep struggling with this issue in my life." God says, *"I'm patient. I'll work with you."*

You may say, "I'm so selfish. I just think about myself

all the time." God says, *"I think about you all the time as well. You're special to me."*

Ask God to show you how much he loves you. Listen carefully to his still, small voice, and remember that God is love.

Prayer: *Father, help me see just how much you love me. Show me your love in a very special and unique way.*

Love Is Unconditional

God's love for us is unconditional. His love is not based on our performance, our goodness, or anything we can or can't do. His love is a gift, freely given to us. All we have to do is receive it.

"What about sin? Doesn't sin separate us from God?"

I believe there was a time when sin did separate us from God. Scripture confirms this:

> *But your iniquities have separated you from your God; and your sins have hidden His face from you, so that he will not hear.* (Isaiah 59:2)

Before Jesus came to earth, people lived under a different agreement or different covenant with God. Their sins were held against them. The High Priest would perform continual sacrifices to deal with the sins of the people. Until Christ came, sin separated people from God.

Today, we live under a new agreement, and Jesus—our new High Priest—died once for all of our sins. Here's how the writer of Hebrews describes it:

> *Under the old covenant, the priest stands before the altar day after day, offering sacrifices that can never take away sins. But our High Priest (Jesus) offered himself to God as **one sacrifice for sins, good for all time**. Then he sat down at the place*

of highest honor at God's right hand. (Hebrews 10:11, 12, emphasis mine)

Did you catch that? Jesus died as "one sacrifice for sins, good for all time." Paul explains it this way, *"God was reconciling the world to himself in Christ, not counting men's sins against them"* (2 Corinthians 5:19). Jesus died for your sins, once and for all. They are dealt with completely. Your past sins, your present sins, and your future sins are no longer counted against you.

This is great news! Now, there is nothing that can separate you from God's love.

> *For I am persuaded that neither death nor life, nor angels nor principalities nor powers, nor things present nor things to come, nor height nor depth, nor any other created thing, shall be able to separate us from the love of God which is in Christ Jesus our Lord.* (Romans 8:38, 39)

Nothing can separate you from God's love. Nothing. He made a way for you to come to him just as you are. What's holding you back?

> *Let us therefore come boldly to the throne of grace that we may obtain mercy and find grace to help in time of need.* (Hebrews 4:16)

Paul Ellis explains it this way: "The only thing that can come between you and his love is your refusal to receive it. The only thing that can separate you from the love of

God is you."[x]

I encourage you to come boldly before the throne of grace in your time of need. Jesus made a way for you to do that. God is ready to receive you, with his arms open wide and a loving smile on his face. He wants you to come running into his arms. He loves you more than you know.

There's nothing you can do to disappoint God.

Prayer: *Father, show me how much you love me. I come to you right now just as I am. Receive me into your arms of love.*

Love Is Giving

Take a moment to ponder the words of Jesus:

> ...*It is more blessed to give than to receive.* (Acts 20:35b)

God is such a giving God. He loves to give and give and give. He never takes away—he only gives.

> *Every good gift and every perfect gift is from above, and comes down from the Father of lights.* (James 1:17)

I think about Matthew 6 where Jesus encourages us not to worry:

> *Therefore I say to you, do not worry about your life, what you will eat or what you will drink; nor about your body, what you will put on. Is not life more than food and the body more than clothing? Look at the birds of the air, for they neither sow nor reap nor gather into barns; yet your heavenly Father feeds them. Are you not of more value than they? Which of you by worrying can add one cubit to his stature? So why do you worry about clothing?*

> *Consider the lilies of the field, how they grow: they neither toil nor spin; and yet I say to you that even Solomon in all his glory was not arrayed like one of these. Now if God so clothes*

*the grass of the field, which today is, and
tomorrow is thrown into the oven, will he not
much more clothe you, O you of little faith?
Therefore do not worry, saying, 'What shall we
eat?' or 'What shall we drink?' or 'What shall we
wear?' For after all these things the Gentiles seek.
For your heavenly Father knows that you need all
these things. (v. 25-32)*

Your heavenly Father knows what you need—mentally,
physically, emotionally, and financially. Not only that,
he wants to give you what you need. He loves to give
you what you need. The key, however, is the next verse:

*But seek first the kingdom of God and His
righteousness, and all these things shall be added
to you. (Matthew 6:33)*

When you put God first in your pursuits—whatever
they may be—then he'll give you what you need. Why?
Because he loves you so much. So much so that Jesus
said we didn't even have to worry about that stuff.

Amazingly, it doesn't stop with earthly things. God has
so much in store for us regarding heavenly things.

*Do not fear, little flock, for it is your Father's
good pleasure to give you the kingdom. (Luke
12:32)*

Did you catch that? It's God's good pleasure to give us
the Kingdom. Take a moment and let that sink in.

Because we are his children, we have inherited something great! As a child of the King, we have been given the Kingdom of God!

What are you lacking in your life—peace, hope, finances, provision, relationships? Take a few moments to reread those verses above. They are truth. They are God's promises to us. God has promised to give us what we need to live at peace.

Prayer: *Father, help me understand all that you have given me in Christ.*

Love Is Powerful

If we can fully understand just how much God loves us, it will cast out all fear.

There is no fear in love; but perfect love casts out fear. (1 John 4:18a)

God's love is not a natural love. God's love is powerful.

Too often, when faced with crippling fear or anxiety, we strive hard to find a solution. We read, study, listen, and do things to find that elusive freedom from fear. "I'll try harder, learn more, overcome, beat this thing. I will fight!" Sound familiar?

I did this for years. Even today, I still do to some degree. Sadly, we often turn to other things for temporary freedom—alcohol, cigarettes, busyness, entertainment, sex, and distraction—whatever we can find to numb the fear. We're trying to alleviate a legitimate issue through illegitimate means.

God's love for us is supernatural—it goes beyond our natural understanding and reasoning. It carries great power; interestingly, when you put your trust in Christ, that same power that raised Jesus from the dead now lives inside of you (Ephesians 1:19-20). You are empowered to live a victorious life.

So, how do I activate that power in my life?

*...the exceeding greatness of His power toward us
who believe.* (Ephesians 1:19)

This exceedingly great power is activated when we
believe.

Let me give you another example in Scripture. Most
believers are familiar with Ephesians 3:20, *"God is able
to do exceedingly abundantly above all we can ask or
think."* Sounds awesome, doesn't it? The problem is that
we don't quote the whole Scripture. We stop too soon.
Here's the entire Scripture:

> *Now to Him who is able to do exceedingly
> abundantly above all that we ask or think,
> **according to the power that works in us**.*
> (Ephesians 3:20, emphasis mine)

The words "according to" indicate a limitation. For
example, if I say, "You can play the piano *according to*
your ability," it implies that you can only play to the
limit of your ability. Or, another example, "You can run
according to your fitness level." Again, the words
"according to" indicate that you can only run at a
certain fitness level.

God's power—that he can do exceedingly, abundantly
above all we can ask or think—is limited to what we
believe (Ephesians 1:19).

Do you believe God wants you free from fear? Do you
believe you can be victorious? Do you believe you can

do things that you previously could not?

For years, I believed I was trapped in fear and could not get free. I believed it was too big, too much, too hard. God could not work in my life because I limited him through what I believed. His power was limited because it is released "according to" what I believed.

Today, I believe with all my heart that God wants us to be free from fear. He is fighting for us constantly, continually, around the clock, 24/7. He wants you free from fear more than you want to be free. However, he is limited through our faith, through what we believe.

I encourage you to believe that God is for you, not against you. He's fighting for your freedom. Believe it. The power to set you free is already inside you through Christ. When we believe, God is able to do exceedingly, abundantly above all we can ask or think, according to that power!

Prayer: *Father, I believe. I believe that your power is inside of me, and I believe that you are fighting for me, to set me free. Release your freedom power inside of me.*

Love Is Peaceful

When I think of God's love towards us, I think about the Christmas story—the night Jesus was born in Bethlehem. Imagine being a shepherd that night, and try to imagine this incredible event unfolding before you as an angel of the Lord comes to deliver a message:

> *Now there were in the same country shepherds living out in the fields, keeping watch over their flock by night. And behold, an angel of the Lord stood before them, and the glory of the Lord shone around them, and they were greatly afraid. Then the angel said to them, "Do not be afraid, for behold, I bring you good tidings of great joy which will be to all people. For there is born to you this day in the city of David a Savior, who is Christ the Lord. And this will be the sign to you: You will find a Babe wrapped in swaddling cloths, lying in a manger."*
>
> *And suddenly there was with the angel a multitude of the heavenly host praising God and saying: "Glory to God in the highest, And on earth peace, goodwill toward men!"*
>
> *So it was, when the angels had gone away from them into heaven, that the shepherds said to one another, "Let us now go to Bethlehem and see this thing that has come to pass, which the Lord has*

made known to us." And they came with haste and found Mary and Joseph, and the Babe lying in a manger. Now when they had seen Him, they made widely known the saying which was told them concerning this Child. And all those who heard it marveled at those things which were told them by the shepherds. (Luke 2:8-18)

It's late one night, and you're tending to your flock. All of sudden, an angel appears!

What's even more amazing is what happens after this angel delivers his message. *Suddenly there was with the angel a multitude of the heavenly host praising God and saying: "Glory to God in the highest, and on earth peace, goodwill toward men!"*

Suddenly, heaven opens up and a bunch of angels appear, speaking in unison, "Glory to God in the highest, and on earth peace, goodwill toward men!" This heavenly declaration must have been very important, that God would send a host of angels to declare it.

It was very important, and, sadly, I think most of us miss the real message of what they said. We've heard this story so many times around the Christmas holidays. We sing songs about it. We talk about it in Christmas stories. We glaze over it and often miss the real message of what the angels were declaring.

They were **not** saying, "Tonight a Savior is born and he's bringing world peace." Rather, the angels were declaring God's new attitude toward us because of what Jesus accomplished on the cross. All of God's punishment and wrath was taken care of. He no longer looked at us with judgment, shame, or anger. Because of Christ, our Father now looks at us with peace and goodwill. That's why the angels declared, "on earth peace, goodwill towards men."

The heavenly message that night was simply this: Because of this child who is born today, everything changes. God's thoughts toward people here on earth are now thoughts of peace and goodwill. They are good thoughts, peaceful thoughts, hopeful thoughts.

What a message of love!

This Christmas season, I encourage you to think about this story of the shepherds in the pastures that night. However, think about the message they heard from the angels—a message of hope and peace. A message that God loves us so much that he sent his only Son to die for us and give us eternal life.

Prayer: *Thank you for sending your Son to die for us. Thank you that your thoughts toward us are thoughts of peace, not of evil, to give us a future and hope (Jeremiah 29:11-14).*

Love Restores Glory

I read this message from Joseph Prince[xi] that really touched my heart. It's yet another beautiful demonstration of God's love towards us:

And the glory which You gave Me I have given them, that they may be one just as We are one. (John 17:22)

The Bible says that God crowned man with glory and honor (Psalm 8:5). The word "crowned" here means to surround or to encompass like a circle. Man's clothing was the glory of God.

According to Romans 3:23, when man sinned, he forfeited the glory. The glory of God came back down when Jesus was born (Luke 2:9). Before his death, Jesus said, "The glory which You gave Me I have given them, that they may be one just as We are one."

Jesus, therefore, restored the glory to man. This came about when Jesus died on the cross.

So, what exactly is God's glory? The Greek word for glory is "*doxa.*" It means having an opinion concerning someone, which results in honor, praise, and glory. God wants us to understand that we are praiseworthy, honorable, and glorious because of his good opinion of us. This came about because Jesus restored glory.

Have you noticed that people's spirits are lifted around

you? There is something that impacts others when they are around you.

God's glory is able to touch every area of your life—your finances, work, relationships, and your health. You can walk in divine health.

Heed the Scripture that states: Arise and Shine! (Isaiah 60:1)

Remember, Jesus gave us his righteousness and restored the glory of God to us.

Prayer: *Father, please help me to understand your gifts and to receive all of your love.*

Love Is Rest

While in the midst of crippling fear and anxiety, I would often think God was not pleased with me. If he were pleased with me, then surely he would take this fear away. Surely, he would pour out peace and give me a strong mind.

Nevertheless, the fear kept coming, so I assumed God was not happy with me. Maybe it was sin. Maybe it was my thought life. Maybe I didn't spend enough quiet time with God. What could I do to please him?

The more I searched—what can I do to please God?—the more I realized that there is nothing I can do to please God. He is perfect. He requires perfection. He is a holy God. His standard of righteousness is beyond my reach. There is nothing I can do to be holy or worthy. This fact is even confirmed in Scripture.

> *There is none righteous, no, not one.* (Romans 3:10)

This is not good news.

All that was compounded by this gnawing sensation that something was wrong with me. Why couldn't I do better? Why couldn't I spend more time with God? Why couldn't I overcome this bad habit? Why couldn't I shake this feeling of fear? What was wrong with me?

I was really feeling hopeless.

That gnawing sensation, I learned later, was shame. Moreover, it was relentless. It made me feel bad, and it never let up. It was a constant voice in my head that told me I wasn't good enough, or that I would never be good enough.

People who struggle with shame have one of two responses. Either they constantly beat themselves up by trying harder to please God only to fail, or they just give up the notion of being good altogether and choose to rebel.

Neither of those responses is good nor healthy. In fact, they are quite destructive.

So, is there hope? Yes!

The answer is twofold. First, you do please God, and second, there is no more shame.

First, you please God in Christ. Those thoughts I had about displeasing God—my sins, my failures—were not from God. If you have truly put your faith in Christ and believe him, then you please God right now, no matter what you're going through. The divine exchange happened when you believed. All of your sins were taken off you and put on Christ at the Cross. In addition, all of Jesus' righteousness was put on you. Now, your sins are remembered no more (Hebrews 8:12). You are declared a child of God (1 John 3:1). The Father has given you his Kingdom (Luke 12:32). In

Christ, you please God!

Secondly, the shame of all your sins—past, present, and future—is gone. Jesus took all your shame on the Cross. The reason we experience shame today is that we don't believe we are free from sin. We strive to please God in our own strength and efforts, and fail because God's standard is perfection. We don't realize that our efforts to please God do nothing but hurt us and hinder us. They are like filthy rags (Isaiah 64:6).

When we try to please God in our own strength and our own efforts, we are saying that Christ's death on the cross is not enough. We need to do more.

Romans 4:4 declares that gifts are given freely and wages are earned and that eternal life is a gift. We cannot earn it. Galatians 2:6 also confirms that no flesh shall be justified (made right with God) by our efforts and our works.

Do you know what pleases God? The Bible says in Hebrews 11:6 that faith pleases God. In other words, when we believe (faith) that we are righteous through the works of Christ and not through our efforts and strength, then God is pleased with us.

I have found incredible peace and freedom in this truth. All of my striving, my work, and my efforts to please God are gone. I please him right now, as I am! He's happy with me!

Prayer: *Father, show me that I am righteous and justified by what I believe, not what I do. Show me that I am pleasing to you in Christ.*

Love Makes Us Whole

Recently, I've been studying this Scripture:

*For by grace you have been saved through faith,
and that not of yourselves; it is the gift of God.*
(Ephesians 2:8)

I've heard this Scripture for years. So much so, that I've become quite familiar with it, but familiarity breeds complacency. The more we know something, the less importance we give it. I call it the "curse of knowledge."

Each day this week as I said those words, something started to stir my soul. I began to realize that incredible freedom lies in the truth of these words. Freedom from fear, anxiety, torment, and panic attacks is right there in these words.

Let me show you.
- By grace
- You have been saved
- Through faith

By Grace

Righteousness is a gift from God. It's not something we can earn or work for. In Romans 4, Paul contrasts the difference between a wage and a gift:

*Now to him who works, the wages are not
counted as grace but as debt. But to him who*

does not work but believes on Him who justifies
the ungodly, his faith is accounted for
righteousness. (Romans 4:4-5)

When you work for your right-standing with God, then it's accounted to you as a wage. The problem is that God requires perfection, so the wage becomes a debt against you that you'll never be able to pay. None of us will ever be able to meet his requirements for righteousness, but he knew that, and he sent his Son to take our sin and give us his righteousness (2 Corinthians 5:21). The divine exchange.

You Have Been Saved

The gift is salvation, but again, we are so familiar with this word. Do we really know what it means to be saved? What are we saved from?

To fully understand what it means, let's go to the original language of the New Testament. This word "saved" comes from the Greek word "*sozo*" (sode'-zo). This word literally means "to be made whole in our body, soul, and spirit."

Salvation is so much more than just being saved from hell. Jesus didn't just die to keep you out of hell—he died to make you whole (Isaiah 53:4-5), give you freedom (John 8:32), and give you abundant life (John 10:10).

Fear, panic, depression, and anxiety are often the results

of deep emotional wounds and trauma. You need to know that Jesus died to set you free from those crippling things, so that you can live life abundantly, in every area of your life.

Through Faith

Like the word "saved," I believe we have also become too familiar with this word "faith." We've given it a variety of meanings and variations. She's of this faith and he's of that faith. If I just had more faith, then surely God would respond to my prayers.

Again, let me go back to the original language. This word "faith" comes from the Greek word "*pistis*." Throughout the New Testament, it is translated as "faith." Interestingly, the verb variation of this word is "*pisteuo*," which is translated as "believe." The word "faith" in the New Testament simply means belief or believing. To have faith is simply to believe.

Now, combine these three phrases: By grace, you have been saved, through faith.

Here's my paraphrase: When you can truly believe that righteousness in Christ is a gift from God, you will be made whole in your body, soul, and spirit.

This is such truth to me. I have experienced deeper levels of freedom and peace knowing that God is pleased with me. I can now boldly come into the throne of grace in my time of need (Hebrews 4:16) and talk to

God as my Father. I don't have to strive and strain to please him. He's happy with me just as I am, because he has given me a new heart (Ezekiel 36:26).

Prayer: *Father, help me understand more and more how, by grace, I have been saved through faith.*

PART V

Changing the Way You Think

Our brains are these amazing, complex creations, and it's only in recent years that scientists have truly begun to understand these biological neural networks God created in our brains to help us adjust, adapt, and learn. Sadly, the enemy knows this and has used it against us since the fall.

I read a great book called *Escaping the Matrix: Setting Your Mind Free to Experience Real Life in Christ* by Pastor Greg Boyd and neuroscientist Al Larson. They describe the wonderful complexities of the human mind and brain but also share how the enemy has used our own minds against us. That's why we are reminded in scripture to renew our minds:

> *Don't copy the behavior and customs of this world, but let God transform you into a new person by changing the way you think. Then you will learn to know God's will for you, which is good and pleasing and perfect.* (Romans 12:2)

Instead, there must be a spiritual renewal of your thoughts and attitudes. (Ephesians 4:23)

While that may feel impossible for those struggling with crippling fear, anxiety, and panic attacks, it is possible to change the way you think and the way you respond. God would not instruct us to do something that we can't do.

Let's start with the word "repent." Take a moment and think about that word. What does it mean to you? Use it in a sentence that you hear often. Does it sound something like this?

- Repent of your sins.
- Repent and turn away from bad decisions.
- When you sin, you need to repent.
- Stop sinning and start doing good.

Any of those sound familiar? Well, honestly, those are a wrong use of the word "repent."

Repentance, in the original language, is not turning away from our sins. In fact, when you look through the New Testament and the 32 verses that mention the word "repent" in some form, nowhere does it say "Repent of your sins." It does say

- Repent and believe (Mark 1:15)
- Repent and be baptized (Acts 2:38)
- Repent and be converted (Acts 3:19)
- Repent and turn to God (Acts 26:20)

The word "repent" in the New Testament is the Greek word "*metanoeo.*" It's a combination of two words:

- *meta*: to change (like **meta**morphosis)
- *noieo*: the mind, our "thinker" (like the word **know**ledge)

"To repent" literally means "to change the way you think." Jesus said,

> *Repent, for the kingdom of heaven is at hand.*
> (Matthew 4:17)

He was saying, "Stop thinking the old way and think a new way, the way God wants you to think." He was simply saying, "Think differently."

There is a new way to think about the Kingdom of heaven and God's plan for us.

Prayer: *Father, help me think differently. Help me to renew my mind and open my heart to the truth of what you want to speak into my life.*

The Unseen Spiritual World

*You're here because you know something. What
you know you can't explain. But you feel it.
You've felt it your entire life...There's something
wrong with the world. You don't know what it is,
but it's there, like a splinter in your mind driving
you mad. It is this feeling that has brought you to
me. Do you know what I'm talking about?*

— Morpheus in *The Matrix*

In the movie *The Matrix*, Morpheus invites Neo into
this journey of truth. For his entire life, Neo had been
blinded from the true world around him. Something
was gnawing at him, drawing him to want to know the
truth. He was easily convinced to take that step from
death to life and soon entered the world of the Matrix.

In many ways, this modern-day parable illustrates an
incredible biblical truth—we too were born in this
world, blinded to the real, spiritual world around us.
We have grown accustomed to the "patterns" and
"behaviors" of this world (Romans 12:1, 2). Even more,
our computer-like brains have been specifically
programmed by this world. Through media, education,
and the choices we make, our patterns of thinking have
been programmed like a computer.

Interestingly, our minds were created by God to be

infused with truth, wisdom, and godly principles; however, the god of this world (2 Corinthians 4:4), Satan, has used this God-given ability against us. Instead of our minds being programmed correctly with Truth, the enemy has programmed our minds with lies and deception.

> *[Satan] was a murderer from the beginning and has always hated the truth. There is no truth in him. When he lies, it is consistent with his character; for he is a liar and the father of lies.* (John 8:44)

All fear, anxiety, depression and panic attacks are rooted in lies. We must replace those crippling lies with God's Truth. When we do,

> *The peace of God, which surpasses all understanding, will guard your hearts and minds through Christ Jesus.* (Philippians 4:7)

We must recognize that "we are not human beings having a spiritual experience, but spiritual beings having a human experience."[xii] Like Neo in **The Matrix**, we must come to know that this world is subject to a greater, more real world around us—the unseen spiritual world.

This can be difficult. As we are born into this world, we are taught, wrongly, that it's the only world that's real. The onslaught of media, culture, education, and upbringing solidifies these lies so that believing in a spiritual world can be near impossible. Our world is immersed in unbelief, and so few people can simply believe.

Thankfully, God is on our side, and he wants to help. He has sent the Holy Spirit to teach us and guide us into all truth (John 14:26). No matter how your mind has been programmed, or what lies have controlled your life up until now, God has both the desire and the power to transform your thinking. Our job is to simply submit ourselves to him. By yielding your mind and soul to the Holy Spirit, you can start the transformation process today. We can renew our minds with the truth, and when we know the truth, it will set us free (John 8:32).

Prayer: *Father, I surrender my soul and my mind to your Holy Spirit. Teach me more about the Truth in Christ and about the real spiritual world to which you've called us.*

Lies and Deception

As believers battling anxiety, panic attacks, and fear, we often struggle with this incredibly frustrating tension between biblical truth and our own experiences. See if any of these sound familiar:

My experience: I haven't been able to conquer these fears. They seem constantly to be conquering me.
Biblical truth: We are more than conquerors in Christ (Romans 8:37).

My experience: My life sure doesn't feel abundant. In fact, it feels quite restricted because of fears and anxiety.
Biblical truth: Jesus came to give life and life more abundantly (John 10:10).

My experience: I can't do all things. I've tried over and over, but the fear is too strong.
Biblical truth: I can do all things through Christ who gives me strength (Philippians 4:13).

My experience: I don't feel very loving. I don't seem to have any power over this. In addition, my mind does not feel very sound. I'm confused and scared.
Biblical truth: You have not been given a spirit of fear, but of love, power and a sound mind (2 Timothy 1:7).

I still struggle to reconcile many of God's truths with my own experiences. It's the battle we constantly wage in our minds. If God's word is true, then why doesn't it seem to be true in my life?

We have this unseen world around us that bombards our minds and thoughts with lies and deception. The Bible talks about this "world" that we live in. It's not referring directly to this physical earth—rather, it's referencing this world system, the patterns and ways of thinking. I like how Greg Boyd describes it:

> [The world system] is an evil system (Galatians 1:4) that has its own wisdom (1 Corinthians 2:6), its own standards (1 Corinthians 3:18), its own earthly and spiritual rulers (1 Corinthians 2:6, 8), and it is ultimately controlled by the "god of this age" (2 Corinthians 4:4, 1 John 5:19).[xiii]

I also like how John Trench describes this "world system" as a "floating mass of thoughts, opinions, maxims, speculations, hopes, impulses, aims, aspirations...which constitute a most real and effective power, being the moral or immoral atmosphere which at every moment of our lives we inhale."[xiv]

I believe the primary reason we struggle to connect God's truth with our own experiences is that our minds are programmed, conformed, and patterned by this world system. Through lies and deceptions, the "god of this age" has successfully blinded many minds from God's truth through improper programming.

Nevertheless, there's hope. All things are possible with

God (Matthew 19:26). If God instructs us to "no longer conform to the patterns of this world, but be transformed by the renewing of our mind" (Romans 12:2), then he'll provide a way for that to happen. He would never tell us to do something we couldn't do.

In her book *Who Switched Off My Brain?* Dr. Caroline Leaf talks about how our brains are physically wired by experiences—both good and bad. Bad experiences produce bad branches within our brains and good experiences produce good branches. However, these branches in our brains are not permanent. By transforming our thoughts and renewing our minds, we can tear down those bad branches and build up the good ones. We can rebuild our patterns of thinking so that God's truths will work powerfully in our lives.

Prayer: *Father, help me understand which of these bad branches in my brain are producing fear, anxiety, and panic attacks. Show me how to transform and renew my mind in Christ.*

Brain Power

Our brains are amazing! At a mere three and a half pounds, our little organic computers consist of more than ten billion neurons communicating with one another through more than ten trillion synaptic connections.

The electrical activity in your brain is incredible. It's estimated that your brain processes a hundred million bits of information per second, but its reticular activating system deletes 98% of the information that is not necessary. Of the remaining two million bits of information that are allowed to pass through per second, your brain only allows five to nine pieces of information to surface to your conscious awareness. That is how decisions are made, memories are remembered, and situations are experienced.

The electrical signals moving through your brain form patterns, or neural nets, based on a variety of input like trauma, education, emotion, memories, and life experiences. In most cases, we are not conscious of these neural nets that are programmed into our brains.

Pastor Boyd and neurologist Al Larson note that "[s]omeone or something installed these for you. And since your whole sense of reality is rooted in these neural-nets, it follows that your whole sense of reality at any given moment has been largely determined by other people and outside events."[xv]

For those struggling with anxiety or fear, traumatic neural nets are often the cause. Something we experienced or learned as a child often triggers these neural nets into a fear response. As soon as we get into a situation that triggers that "stronghold of fear," our bodies and minds switch to autopilot and fear rises up within us. For most, it happens subconsciously, and we don't have time to respond and think logically through the experience. It becomes a reaction instead of an action.

But there is hope. God has given us the power to remove those unhealthy neural nets and replace them with godly programming. He not only wants us to be free, he has given us his Holy Spirit to help us walk into freedom.

> *Do not be conformed to this world, but **be transformed by the renewing of your mind**, that you may prove what is that good and acceptable and perfect will of God.* (Romans 12:2, emphasis mine)

God would not instruct us to be "transformed by the renewing of our mind" if it weren't possible. It is possible! We can work through these negative, destructive patterns of thinking, and replace them with godly ways of thinking. Those triggers of fear, anxiety, and panic attacks can be removed and torn down. We can learn to take every thought captive. God has given us spiritual weapons to tear down these strongholds, these patterns of thinking:

> *For the weapons of our warfare are not carnal but mighty in God for pulling down strongholds, casting down arguments and every high thing that exalts itself against the knowledge of God, bringing every thought into captivity to the obedience of Christ.* (2 Corinthians 10:4-5)

Ask God to help you recognize any negative or destructive "patterns of thinking" and ask the Holy Spirit to guide you into truth, because you shall know the truth, and the truth shall set you free (John 8:32).

Prayer: *Father, show me any wrong patterns of thinking and let the power of Christ in me tear down those strongholds.*

It Is Finished

Now that we've laid a solid foundation about the importance of renewing our minds, I want to spend time talking about specific areas of our thinking processes that need to be renewed. It's very important to understand those areas of our thinking that are not established in truth, because when we know the truth, the truth will set us free (John 8:32).

I want to focus on **the finished work of Christ**.

Right before Jesus died on the cross, he said something very profound that many of us miss or fail to really understand. He said,

> *It is finished.* (John 19:30)

What exactly was finished? What work did he do that he no longer needed to do? Moreover, how does that affect us?

When Jesus died on the cross, he fulfilled all the righteous requirements of the law (Matthew 5:13). Once he died and fulfilled all the requirements of the Law, there was nothing left for us to do to earn right-standing with God.

He ushered in a New Covenant, a new agreement with God. What exactly is this new agreement?

It is simply this:

> *If you confess with your mouth the Lord Jesus
> and believe in your heart that God has raised
> Him from the dead, you will be saved.* (Romans
> 10:9)

Salvation is no longer a result of following rules and regulations—salvation now comes through faith in Christ, putting all your hope and trust in him to save you.

When you can truly understand and receive God's forgiveness, it will bring healing and restoration to your entire body, soul, and spirit. There is amazing wholeness that comes through understanding God's forgiveness and being able to forgive others. In receiving and giving forgiveness, you will find healing for your soul and for your body.

One prominent area of our mind that needs renewing is the area of forgiveness. We must truly understand that God is so passionately and wonderfully in love with us that he made a way through his Son, Jesus, to wipe away our sins. In addition, the reason he did that was to remove the barrier that would keep us from coming to him. That is why we can now *"come boldly to the throne of grace in our time of need"* (Hebrews 4:16).

When Jesus died on the cross, he died for your sins. All of them. Past sins, present sins, and future sins—they are all gone.

Consider these promises:

- For the death that [Jesus] died, He died to sin once for all (Romans 6:10).

- "I will never again remember their sins" (Hebrews 8:12).

- He is faithful and just to forgive us our sins and to cleanse us from all unrighteousness (1 John 1:9).

Today, I encourage you to spend some time with God, asking him to renew your mind in this area and to help you understand this truth of the finished work of Christ. Ask him to teach you and guide you into this powerful, life-changing truth: your freedom is already finished and available to you today.

Prayer: *Father, open up my heart and mind to fully understand the finished work of Christ and all that's available to me today.*

God Is Not Punishing Me

We've all made mistakes. Many of us feel guilty for those mistakes, and according to God's righteous requirements, all sin must be punished.

If we stopped right now, this message would not be very encouraging. All have sinned and all sin must be punished. But thankfully, that's not the end of the story.

By God's wisdom and glorious plan, he did punish sin. All sin. Jesus was afflicted, bruised, beaten, and punished for our sins. Read these words:

Surely he has borne our griefs and carried our sorrows;
Yet we esteemed Him stricken, smitten by God, and afflicted.

But he was wounded for our transgressions,
He was bruised for our iniquities;
The chastisement for our peace was upon Him,
And by His stripes we are healed.

All we like sheep have gone astray; we have turned, every one, to his own way;
And the LORD has laid on Him the iniquity of us all.

He was oppressed and he was afflicted, yet he opened not His mouth;
He was led as a lamb to the slaughter, and as a

sheep before its shearers is silent,
So he opened not His mouth.

Yet it pleased the LORD to bruise Him... (Isaiah
53:4-7, 10a)

Did you catch that? "The Lord has laid on Him the
iniquity of us all." All of our punishment was put on
Christ. This punishment "pleased the Lord." Why was
God pleased to afflict Christ? So that you would be free
to come to the Father, completely free from sin in your
time of need (Hebrews 4:16).

What's left for us? Grace!

When you start to think that your anxiety, fear, or bad
choices are the result of God's punishment, you must
stop and renew your mind to know that God is not
punishing you. There is no punishment left for you.

Prayer: *Father, help me renew my mind to know that*
you are with me, not against me. Reveal to me your
grace!

I Can Overcome Fear

Too many times, fear screams so loud and rears its ugly head, and we so often respond to it. We give in. We obey the fear. Nevertheless, here's how the Bible encourages us to stand against this "roaring lion":

Stay alert! Watch out for your great enemy, the devil. He prowls around like a roaring lion, looking for someone to devour. (1 Peter 5:8)

Fear is just a voice, a roaring voice in your mind that exaggerates circumstances. When the devil lies to us and tries to create fear, we should stand against those lies. Listen how the very next verse encourages us to respond to those fearful threats:

Stand firm against him, and be strong in your faith. Remember that your Christian brothers and sisters all over the world are going through the same kind of suffering you are. (1 Peter 5:9)

Phrases like "stand firm" and "be strong" imply that you can do this. Scripture confirms that we will not be given a temptation beyond what we can bear.

The temptations in your life are no different from what others experience. And God is faithful. He will not allow the temptation to be more than you can stand. When you are tempted, he will show

you a way out so that you can endure. (1
Corinthians 10:13)

According to this verse, you will always have a "way out
so that you can endure." This is a great promise from
God!

I know how unbearable fear and panic can feel at times.
When your body responds with heart palpitations, your
breathing gets shallow, and your hands and feet start
tingling, it can feel incredibly overwhelming.
Nevertheless, you can rest in the truth of God's
promises and not give in to the fear. You can *"stand still
and see the salvation of God"* (Exodus 14:13).

The key to overcoming fear is to look to Christ. He is
your salvation—not just for heaven, but for life here on
earth as well. Listen carefully to the words of Jesus:

> *I have told you all this so that you may have
> peace in me. Here on earth you will have many
> trials and sorrows. But take heart, because I have
> overcome the world.* (John 16:31)

In a very straightforward way, Jesus said we will have
"many trials and sorrows." I'm so glad he didn't stop
there. "Take heart!" he said. Be encouraged. Why?
Because he overcame this crazy, fearful, unpredictable
world.

If you want to overcome fear, look to Jesus. He will
carry you through those fearful times!

Prayer: *Father, help me renew my mind so that I may know I can overcome any fear that roars against me. I put all my trust in you.*

I Can Be Free

During times of confusion, the enemy will often whisper into your ear, "You'll never be free."

It's just not true. God's desire for you is freedom. Total, complete freedom. He never created you to suffer, to experience fear, to be crippled by anxiety. Listen carefully to words of Christ:

> *The thief does not come except to steal, and to kill, and to destroy. I have come that they may have life, and that they may have it more abundantly.* (John 10:10)

Here are some steps to help you renew your mind that freedom is possible:

Believe that Freedom Is Possible

Jesus said in Matthew 19:26, "...with God all things are possible." God is for you, and he wants you to be free. He sent Christ into this world to help you live the abundant life. He died a painful, brutal death so that you can have life. He paid an incredible price for your freedom.

Seek First the Kingdom of God

Sometimes when the fear and anxiety strike hard, we immediately seek a solution to our pain. That's a very natural response. However, where we often fall short is seeking God for an answer. Matthew 6:33 encourages us to "seek first the Kingdom of God," and all those things that create anxiety in us will fade away. Instead of reaching out to God as a last resort, let him be your first response.

Worship

I believe worship is at the heart of God. He doesn't call us to worship so he can feel good about himself; rather, he calls us to worship for our own sakes. Worship is an act of surrender, and often fear and panic are the result of our attempts to maintain control, but the more we surrender our lives through worship, the more God's power sweeps in and gives us strength. In addition, worship opens up our hearts to hear God more clearly.

Listen with Your Heart

Freedom comes when we hear God with our hearts. I have heard numerous stories about people who take time to listen to God, and when he "speaks," freedom is almost instant.

> *Faith comes by hearing, and hearing by the Word of God.* (Romans 10:17)

Take time to listen to God, and learn how to hear him.

Prayer: *Father, reveal to my heart that freedom is possible. Teach me how to receive all that you have for me in Christ.*

I Am God's Child

Now I want to focus on a very important truth: in Christ, you are God's child.

> *To all who believed him and accepted [Jesus], he gave the right to become children of God.* (John 1:12)

We've probably heard this numerous times, and we may even say to ourselves, *I'm a child of God.* However, what does that mean? How does it apply to my life? How can it help me overcome this tormenting fear and anxiety?

If we can get this concept from our minds (understanding) into our hearts (believing), I am convinced that it will bring freedom and deliverance. To help you understand what this means, here are some benefits of being a child of God:

We Are Joint Heirs with Christ

> *The Spirit Himself bears witness with our spirit that we are children of God, and if children, then heirs—heirs of God and joint heirs with Christ, if indeed we suffer with Him, that we may also be glorified together.* (Romans 8:16-17)

What does it mean to be a "joint heir"? Let me give you an example of what joint ownership means. My wife and I have a joint banking account. This account is owned by both of us. We both have access to it. Either of us can make deposits or withdrawals. We jointly own this account. In the same way, all of the promises and blessings that the Father has given to Christ also belong to us—promises of love, joy, peace, patience, kindness, goodness, faithfulness, gentleness, and self-control (Galatians 5:22-23).

We Have Access to the Throne of God

Let us therefore come boldly to the throne of grace that we may obtain mercy and find grace to help in time of need. (Hebrews 4:16)

Because of what Christ has done, we now have full access to the throne of God. When we are struggling, afraid, and confused, we can run boldly to God's throne without fear of wrath or judgment and receive all he has to offer us. Nothing can separate you from the love of God (Romans 8:38-39).

We Are Seated with Christ at the Right Hand of God

God, who is rich in mercy, because of His great love with which he loved us, even when we were dead in trespasses, made us alive together with Christ (by grace you have been saved), and raised us up together, and made us sit together in the heavenly places in Christ Jesus. (Ephesians 2:4-6)

This concept can be difficult to understand, because we live in the realities of this world and with our five senses. We don't feel like we're sitting at the right hand of God. When fear strikes and panic rises up, we don't feel like we're seated in the heavenly realms. Nevertheless, we have to understand that our spirits are with Christ, sealed by the Holy Spirit.

I encourage you to spend some time with God and listen to his "divine whispers" over you. Let him love on you as his child. He loves you so much and wants you to walk in freedom and peace.

Prayer: *Father, show me that I am your child. Show me how much you love me and let me receive all that you have for me in Christ.*

PART VI

Perfect Love Casts Out Fear

I believe grace has the power to cast out fear. As we grow in our knowledge of God's perfect love toward us through grace, it will empower us to find freedom.

> There is no fear in love; but perfect love casts out fear, because fear involves torment. But he who fears has not been made perfect in love. (1 John 4:18)

I've always found this verse a bit cryptic and even condemning at times. The last part made me feel less loved: "he who fears has not been made perfect in love."

I knew I loved God, and I knew he loved me, but I concluded (wrongly) that because I feared, I must have done something to push him away.

As I continue to grow in my walk with God, I'm learning every day just how amazing and powerful grace is. So much of our thinking about God is just plain wrong.

Here are three reasons why I believe our understanding of grace is inaccurate:

Wrong Education

As children, we're often taught (directly and indirectly) that life is all about performance. Do well, and you're rewarded. Do badly, and you're punished. We live in a performance-based culture.

Sadly, most churches today just don't teach the depth of God's grace and what Christ has really done for us. Most messages from the pulpit mix grace with a list of do's and do not's. However, that's not what the Bible says: that grace is a gift freely given, and we can do nothing to earn it.

Wrong Conclusions

Way too often, when the answers don't come, we quickly conclude that God has a different plan for our lives or that our sin is hindering God's working power in the situation. We pray for freedom from fear, but when the next panic attack hits, we start concluding that it's our fault.

- *If I just had more faith...*
- *If I could just overcome this weakness...*
- *If I could just get past this hurt...*
- *If I could just stop sinning...*

Challenge these wrong conclusions. As you grow in

your understanding of God's grace, peace will flood your heart and your mind in Christ Jesus.

We Have an Enemy

We can't forget that there is an unseen enemy who is out to thwart the freedom that grace brings. The more he can confuse and disrupt our grasp of grace, the more he can keep us in bondage.

We should not fear the enemy. Jesus has disarmed him (Colossians 2:15) and has given us authority over Satan and his demons (Luke 10:19).

I encourage you to start thinking about grace. What does it mean to you? How do you define it? How does it apply to your life? Hopefully, we can answer those questions in the upcoming chapters.

Prayer: *Father, help me understand more clearly what I believe about grace. Holy Spirit, teach me about grace and how to apply it to my life.*

Moving from the Old to New Covenant

Grace is amazing! When we can fully grasp the depth of God's grace, it will tear down fear, anger, shame, addictions, and those things that hold us back in life.

To fully understand what grace is and what it can do in our lives, we need to understand the difference between the Old Covenant and the New Covenant.

First, what is a *covenant*? Webster's defines covenant as: *"a written agreement or promise usually under seal between two or more parties especially for the performance of some action."*

A covenant is a binding agreement made between two parties, and biblical covenants are typically sealed through the shedding of blood. Throughout the Bible, there are actually numerous covenants, not just the Old and New. The five most well known biblical covenants are

- Noahic covenant
- Abrahamic covenant
- Mosaic covenant
- Davidic covenant
- New covenant

Under the Old Covenant (the first four listed above), the Law was an agreement between God and people. The priests carried it out, and sacrifices were made for

sin. But the sacrifices never cleansed the people of sin—
they only covered their sin. There were also blessings
for obedience (Deuteronomy 28:1-14) and curses for
disobedience (Deuteronomy 28:15-68). If you did what
was right in God's eyes, you were blessed. If you did
what was wrong, you were cursed.

The New Covenant is a very different agreement. Jesus
became the High Priest (Hebrews 4:14), and offered
himself as the sacrifice. In doing this, he cleansed the
people of their sins, not just covered (Hebrews 9:11-14
and 1 John 1:7). Jesus lived a perfect, sinless life and
thereby fulfilled all the requirements of the law
(Matthew 5:17). Then, he laid down his life as a sin
offering (Hebrews 10:12-14). God accepted it and
declared that those who are in Christ are now children
of God (John 1:12).

Under this New Covenant, our only requirement for
salvation is to *"confess with your mouth the Lord Jesus
and believe in your heart that God has raised Him from
the dead"* (Romans 10:9). There is no Law when we are
"in Christ." Jesus *"takes away the first that he may
establish the second"* (Hebrews 10:9).

Take a moment to think about what this implies:

- The burden to live a perfect life has been fulfilled in
  Christ. It's no longer about us.
- The shame of our sin and mistakes is gone. Christ

took it all upon himself.

- Instead of trying harder to live the Christian life, we can now just enjoy life in Christ.
- Nothing can separate us from the love of God in Christ. Nothing.
- Since it's no longer about us, we are holy, perfect, blameless and righteous in Christ.

There is so much more available to us when we believe this truth about what Christ has accomplished for us. If we can truly grasp what this New Covenant brings, then the pressure to perform is wiped away. We can finally stop living as slaves and start living as children of God.

Prayer: *Father, open my eyes to this truth of grace. Show me that, in Christ, you are pleased with me in every way.*

No Longer a Sinner

Too often, we define ourselves through sin. When we mess up, we verbally and mentally abuse ourselves. *You're so stupid.* Or when we know what to do but don't do it, then we just give up. *Why even try?* This vicious cycle of defeat can be terribly frustrating and create such anxiety and fear in our lives.

Here's how Paul, the apostle, described his own experience with sin: *"I don't really understand myself, for I want to do what is right, but I don't do it. Instead, I do what I hate"* (Romans 7:15). When we are sin-conscious, all we see is our mistakes, our failures, our shortcomings.

The Garden of Eden is a great example of what happens when we move from being God-conscious to self-conscious. Before they sinned, Adam and Eve enjoyed an incredible relationship with God. They walked together in the cool of day (Genesis 3:8) and spent time together. Their fellowship was invigorating and full of life! There was no awareness of sin, no knowledge of right and wrong. There was just fellowship with God.

Then it happened—they ate from the one tree they shouldn't have. Immediately, humanity was aware of good and bad. Sin was birthed. They had become sin-conscious: they were hyper-aware of their failures, mistakes, and shortcomings. So much so that when God showed up, they hid themselves.

> *So he said, "I heard your voice in the garden, and*
> *I was afraid because I was naked; and I hid*
> *myself.* (Genesis 3:10)

The immediate response to sin is shame. When shame sets in, we hide ourselves from God and we become afraid. We often experience fear because we pull away from God due to sin and shame. I don't believe God ever pulls away from us. He will never leave us nor forsake us (Hebrews 13:5). It's always us pulling away from him. Like Adam, we hide ourselves from him because of shame. Moreover, in the same way, God is continually pursuing us because he loves us so much.

From the day Adam and Eve ate from that tree, all of humanity has lived self-consciously and focused on sin—defining ourselves by following rules, doing what is right, and not doing what is wrong. Today, many, many people live this way. However, that's not how God wants us to live.

When Jesus came to earth, he lived a perfect life and then died for our sins; he made a way for us to be sinless in God's eyes. In Christ, we are no longer sinners. In Christ, we are perfect, holy, and righteous. In Christ, we have moved from being sinners to being saints.

But I still sin.

Yes, I do. If you continue reading in Romans 7, Paul

talks about this war in our bodies that wages on continually (v. 23). However, our flesh is not who we are. We are spirit and soul. *"Your real life is hidden with Christ in God"* (Colossians 3:3).

Sin has very real consequences in this life. If you murder, there are consequences. If you steal, there are consequences. If you treat your body poorly, there are consequences. Sin will affect your physical life.

Eric Dykstra says it this way in his book *Grace on Tap*, "In Christ, we are not punished FOR our sins, but we are punished BY our sins."[xvi]

Nevertheless, sin should not define you, because in Christ, God does not see your sin. Honestly, we have it backward.

We think that because of sin, God is not pleased with us, so we try harder not to sin and to clean up our lives. If we can stop sinning for a while, then we can go to God with our needs. We wait to be clean in our own eyes before we approach God. Nevertheless, that's backward.

God says, "You are clean and holy right now in Christ. Come to me as you are and let me help you with those areas of weakness." Strength to stop sinning does not come from us trying harder. It comes from spending time with God and allowing him to help us.

Let us therefore come boldly to the throne of grace that we may obtain mercy and find grace to help in time of need. (Hebrews 4:17)

Prayer: *Father, reveal to me that my sins are gone, washed away, and that I am holy and perfect in your eyes.*

Do I Have a Sinful Nature?

As we continue to grow in our understanding of grace, it is essential that we understand this concept of "sin nature." What is it and how does it apply today? I believe most churches teach a wrong concept of "sin nature," and in doing so, many people are trapped in a fear-based, anxiety-provoking understanding of sin.

What Is a "Sinful Nature"?

The Bible says we are born with a nature to sin—an inward motivation to sin. We don't learn to sin; rather, it comes naturally to us from birth. When we come into this world, our spirits are dead and we must be born again (John 3:3-7).

Today, under the New Covenant, there are only two states of existence: the natural and the spiritual. This is how Paul describes those two states by comparing Adam and Christ in Scripture:

> *The first man was of the earth, made of dust; The second Man is the Lord from heaven.*
>
> *As was the man of dust, so also are those who are made of dust; And as is the heavenly Man, so also are those who are heavenly.*
>
> *And as we have borne the image of the man of dust, we shall also bear the image of the heavenly Man.* (1 Corinthians 15:47-49)

To move from the natural (state of Adam) to the spiritual (state of Christ), you must be born again. Once you are born again by faith, your flesh is crucified with Christ; it is no longer you who lives, but Christ in you (Galatians 2:20).

The Sin Nature Is Dead in Christ

Once you place your faith in Christ, your sin nature dies. You have become alive "in Christ." You are now a new creation:

> *If anyone is in Christ, he is a new creation; old things have passed away; behold, all things have become new.* (2 Corinthians 5:17)

Your old self, your old nature has "passed away." All things "have become new." It's a finished work!

You no longer have a sinful nature. You now have the nature of Christ, not the nature of Adam.

Sinful Nature versus Flesh

Today's modern teaching of the "sinful nature" is based on some recent translations of the Bible. Modern translations like the New International Version (NIV) and New Living Translation (NLT) use the term "sinful nature" throughout the New Testament. However, it's more of an interpretation than a translation. In the King James Version (KJV), New King James Version (NKJV), and New American Standard Bible (NASB), there is no reference to a "sinful nature." It's only in newer translations.

What is this word being interpreted as "sinful nature"?

The Greek word that the NIV and NLT translate as "sinful nature" is the word "*sarx.*" It is defined as the flesh, the meat of an animal, the body (as opposed to the soul or spirit).

The KJV, NKJV, and NASB versions simply translate "*sarx*" as "flesh." It's your body, the natural part of you that experiences this reality through the five senses— taste, touch, smell, sound, and sight. The *flesh* is very different from the *sinful nature.*

Take Romans 7:18, for example, and read both the NIV and the NKJV:

> *I know that nothing good lives in me, **that is, in my sinful nature**. For I have the desire to do what is good, but I cannot carry it out.* (Romans 7:18, NIV, emphasis mine)

> *For I know that in me **(that is, in my flesh)** nothing good dwells; for to will is present with me, but how to perform what is good I do not find.* (Romans 7:18, NKJV, emphasis mine)

Why is this important? Your flesh is this tangible part of you where sin resides. Sin lives in your flesh (Colossians 2:11). However, if you believe that sin is in your soul and spirit—that your nature is to sin—then your identity is all about managing and dealing with sin. Nevertheless, if you can believe that your nature is good, that you are a child of God, then there is hope to live a victorious life. You can conquer the flesh, because Christ did.

Then, why do we still sin? We sin because we believe we should. Phil Drysdale explains it this way, "We still struggle with our old sinful nature because we believe we should. In fact, the reason there is any sin whatsoever in our lives in any area is because we have a framework of belief that empowers it."[xvii]

We continue to sin because we believe that we still have a sin nature. We have to understand that God has somehow uniquely separated our soul and spirit from our body when we become a believer. Our body is dead to sin.

> *If Christ is in you, **the body is dead because of sin,** but the Spirit is life because of righteousness.* (Romans 8:10, emphasis mine)

In Christ, God considers our body dead because of sin. Therefore, we are encouraged to do the same:

> *Consider yourselves dead to sin and alive to God in Christ Jesus.* (Romans 6:11)

We no longer have a sinful nature. It has been crucified and buried with Christ. Our new nature is the nature of Christ, and in him we can overcome fear, anxiety, and panic attacks.

Prayer: *Father, show me that I am a new creation in Christ, that my old sinful nature has been crucified, dead and buried. I am alive in you.*

The Freedom to Laugh and Enjoy Life

One of God's greatest gifts to us is joy. When Jesus died on the cross, he took away all our sins and gave us the opportunity to have a new life—a life of joy and peace, no matter our history.

Grace paves the way for us to experience God's joy!

The World's Joy

I was talking to a woman awhile back who described her childhood as one filled with drinking, partying, and lots of people laughing. As she grew older, she associated these "fun times" with evil behavior. Therefore, in her mind, she wanted to avoid anything resembling that kind of "fun." It became very difficult for her to experience any joy and laughter, because in her mind, anything "fun" was evil. Later in her life, she began to understand this mis-association and started to enjoy life more.

Today, many believers struggle to experience joy in their lives because of this wrong association with fun. Each of us has a desire to experience joy. God put characteristics of himself into each of us. We were made in the image of God (Genesis 1:27), and because of that, God created us to experience joy—and for his own joy. God rejoices over you!

For the LORD your God is living among you.
He is a mighty savior. He will take delight in you
with gladness. With his love, he will calm all your
fears. He will rejoice over you with joyful songs.
(Zephaniah 3:17)

Much of the world's fun and laughter is really just a counterfeit. It is man's attempt to experience what God created us for—to enjoy life. We often strive to fill this legitimate need for joy in an illegitimate way.

A few months ago, I traveled to Las Vegas for work. While I was there, walking around the downtown area, I was mesmerized by all the sights and sounds of Vegas. I had been there many times before, but this visit was different. I began thinking about all the vain promises of Vegas—money, pleasure, and power. Then, it hit me—this is a counterfeit for heaven.

The "joy" of Vegas will always be short-lived and temporary. While it may be fun for a moment, it is not everlasting joy. Only God provides true, everlasting joy. Heaven will be a place of incredible beauty, wealth, and joy.

Here's the incredible truth: we don't need to wait to get to heaven to experience all that God has for us. The Kingdom life that heaven provides is already ours today through faith in Christ. When Jesus said, *"It is finished"* (John 19:30), all of the work required to bring heaven to earth was completed. Paul said it this way, *"[God] has blessed us with every spiritual blessing in the heavenly places in Christ"* (Ephesians 1:3).

It's past tense, a done deal. We are already blessed in Christ. Heaven is ours today!

God's Presence—Cartoons and PB&J

As a worship leader, Steve was familiar with drawing people into the presence of God. Each weekend, he would lead people in worship, and many would experience God's presence and incredible joy.

One Saturday morning, Steve was going through his normal routine. He would make a peanut butter and jelly sandwich and then sit down to watch some Saturday morning cartoons. All of sudden, he felt God's presence. His gut reaction was to stop everything, turn off the TV, and "enter in." However, God whispered to him, "I just want to sit down and watch cartoons with you."

I love this story because it reminds me that God just wants to spend time with us, whatever we're doing no matter how simple or mundane. Even in those little things that bring us joy, he is there, and he wants to draw you into more of those moments of joy and pleasure. Through Christ and his finished work on the cross, there is nothing keeping you from experiencing God's joy, peace, and presence.

Prayer: *Father, help me experience more of your joy. Your kingdom come, your will be done on earth and in my life as it is already in heaven.*

PART VII

How to Pray

When anxious and fearful thoughts come flooding in, it can be very difficult to quiet your mind and connect with God in prayer. In the middle of a panic attack, the last thing on your mind is getting alone with God.

Learning how to pray can calm an anxious mind and fill your heart with peace:

> *Do not be anxious about anything, but in everything, by prayer and petition, with thanksgiving, present your requests to God. And the peace of God, which transcends all understanding, will guard your hearts and your minds in Christ Jesus.* (Philippians 4:6-7)

When anxious thoughts, fear, panic, or worry come against you, present your requests to God. Pray and petition him, and as you do, his peace which goes beyond all understanding will guide your heart and mind in Christ. This is more than just a recommendation—it's a truth that can transform a fearful mind into a mind of peace.

Here are some steps that have helped me connect with God:

Believe

Faith is essential. Without faith, it's impossible to please God (Hebrews 11:6). We must believe that God will respond to our prayers. If we doubt, we are like a wave tossed about by the sea, unsettled in all our ways (James 1:5). Here's how Jesus explains it:

> *Jesus said to the disciples, "Have faith in God. I assure you that you can say to this mountain, 'May God lift you up and throw you into the sea,' and your command will be obeyed. All that's required is that you really believe and do not doubt in your heart. Listen to me! You can pray for anything, and if you believe, you will have it."* (Mark 11:22-24)

God Hears You

I think we've all wondered, "God, do you really hear me?" We pray and pray, and it seems like nothing changes. We hear a thought in our head, *God doesn't hear my prayers,* and we think it's our thought. Quietly, we agree with this subtle attack of the devil. He is the father of lies (John 10:10), and he spews his lies and confusion all over us to thwart God's beautiful plans for our lives. We cannot give into this voice that says God does not hear our prayers. God listens.

Another subtle lie from the enemy is that we are not worthy enough for God to hear our prayers. It's just not true! When you receive Christ, you are instantly made worthy. He took our sins and we took his righteousness.

> *God made [Jesus] who had no sin to be sin for us, so that in him we might become the righteousness of God.* (2 Corinthians 5:21)

Now that you are righteous in Christ, you can boldly come to the throne of grace in your time of need (Hebrews 4:16).

Know who you are in Christ

Too often, we approach God in prayer with a sinner's mentality. "Lord, I'm a wretched sinner. Woe is me! I'm not worthy to come before you." This way of thinking is wrong. Once you receive Christ, you are no longer a slave—you are a child of God!

> *You are no longer a slave but God's own child. And since you are his child, everything he has belongs to you.* (Galatians 4:7)

In Christ, you are a child of the Most High God. You are special! You are cherished, loved, protected, and pursued by God. You are his child!

Words Carry Power

We must be very careful about the words we speak. Words carry incredible spiritual power. Death and life are in the power of our words (Proverbs 18:21). Salvation comes when we confess with our mouths and believe in our hearts (Romans 10:9). Whether good or evil, people speak what's in their hearts. Jesus said it this way,

> *Whatever is in your heart determines what you say. A good person produces good words from a good heart, and an evil person produces evil words from an evil heart.* (Matthew 12:34, 35)

If you want to experience peace, don't speak evil, doubting words. If you feel an anxious thought coming on, don't say, "I'm probably going to have another panic attack." No! Don't speak those words. Rather, pray something like this, "Father, my body feels anxious right now, but you said that you will give me perfect peace when my mind is focused upon you. Right now, Lord, I fix my thoughts upon you. I trust in you!"

Build Your Prayer Muscle

Prayer is a lot like a muscle. You need to work on it, strengthen it, and build it up. Don't wait until you need it to start strengthening it.

A professional athlete doesn't start working out the day before a big race. It takes months and months, even years, to develop the ability to race well. In the same way, we should pray daily, flexing and strengthening our prayer-time muscle.

Physical exercise has some value, but spiritual exercise is much more important, for it promises a reward in both this life and the next. (1 Timothy 4:8)

Prayer: *Father, teach me to pray effectively. Show me how to build and strengthen my prayer muscle so that when anxiety, panic, or fear hits, I can rest in the confidence that you are with me.*

Learning to Rest

One of the biggest challenges for people struggling with anxiety, fear, and panic attacks is the issue of rest.

Rest is essential for us to function normally and effectively. We need rest to clear our heads and to give our bodies the break they need to rejuvenate. There is also a spiritual rest we can experience that will bring incredible freedom and peace. This rest that God talks about is a deep, soulful, soothing rest that helps us live the abundant life Christ died to give us (John 10:10).

Rest for the Body

Physical rest is essential for us to live life abundantly. Failure to rest will result in stress and confusion. It also triggers your adrenaline glands to produce extra energy needed to compensate for the lack of sleep. We also tend to over-caffeinate ourselves when we're tired and exhausted, which also feeds the stress and sleeplessness.

As I've mentioned, I have also found that exercise is wonderful for physical rest. If you have trouble sleeping, then start moving. On the days I trained for my half Ironman triathlon in 2010, I slept so hard and peacefully. Exercise is a wonderful, natural way to regulate your sleep.

Rest for the Soul and Spirit

Hebrews 4 goes into a detailed explanation of this other

"rest" that we can enter into today. It's not referring to physical rest but a mental and spiritual rest.

When the children of Israel were rescued out of Egypt, they were sent on a path to the Promised Land. It was a short journey that should have only taken them a few weeks. However, fear entered their hearts. They saw the land full of giants and danger and did not believe God's promise that he would give them the land. Therefore, they wandered in the wilderness for forty years till everyone died except Joshua and Caleb, the two who believed God.

There's a very important spiritual principle here. The land was theirs by promise. God had given them this land, but they did not believe and missed out on the rest that was theirs for the taking. In the same way, according to Hebrews 4, we too have a rest for the soul and spirit that we can enter into with God. This rest comes from the incredible sacrifice Jesus made for us. He fulfilled the Law and all its requirements (Matthew 5:17) so that we could rest from striving to please God with our works.

In Christ, we are already pleasing to God in every way possible. Jesus became our sin so that we can become righteous, holy, and pleasing to God. There's nothing we can do in our own strength to please God. Nothing. As it says in Hebrews 11:6, the only way to please God is to believe.

So, as it says in Hebrews 4:11, *"let us do our best to enter that rest."*

Prayer: *Father, help me enter into the rest you have for us. Show me how to cease from striving and simply trust you for my salvation.*

The Obedience of Christ

What does it takes to enter into God's rest?

For anyone struggling with anxiety and fear, our relationship with God often feels strained and distant. We pray and plead with God for it to go away. We ask him to give us one day where we don't have to think about fear or possibly have an attack. It can be emotionally and mentally draining. I know because I spent years praying these types of prayers.

Early in my walk with God, I couldn't understand why the fear and panic were so strong. I really desired in my heart to know God better and commit my life to him as best I could. I tried hard to walk in obedience, but I wasn't perfect. Still, I tried. I worked hard to please God. However, I could not find that elusive rest and peace with God.

Today, fear no longer controls my life, and I'm experiencing this incredible depth of rest in God. What's different? Primarily, I have changed the way I relate to God and how he relates to me. Here is what I learned.

It Is Finished

Before Christ, people related to God through the Law, a system of rules and commandments. If you obeyed, God blessed you. If you disobeyed, you were cursed

(Deuteronomy 28). This system of the Law was very clear and had obvious consequences, but it was impossible to keep (Hebrews 8:7-8). Therefore, God set up a sacrificial system to deal with disobedience and sin. People could now relate to him again, but from a distance.

Yet God wanted more than a distant relationship based on rules of right and wrong. He wanted intimacy, where we could come to him as we are and call upon his help in our time of need (Hebrews 4:16). He sent his Son to be the one and only sacrifice for all sin (Hebrews 10:10). It was the perfect sacrifice that takes away the sins of the world (John 1:29). When Jesus died on the Cross, he said, *"It is finished"* (John 19:30).

The covenant of Law was now satisfied in Christ. In addition, a new covenant was established, not based on what we do, but on what we believe (Ephesians 2:8).

Your Sins Are Gone

Your sins are not just forgiven. Every sin—past, present, and future—is gone. God is no longer counting our sins against us (2 Corinthians 5:19). There is no record of your sin. It has been removed from you as far *"as the East is from the West"* (Psalm 103:12). Jesus *"appeared to put away sin by the sacrifice of Himself"* (Hebrews 9:26).

I think one of the key reasons people experience fear is

that they think God is judging them, condemning them, and even punishing them for their mistakes. It's just not true. All judgment, condemnation, and punishment have been taken care of on the Cross. The wrath of God has been satisfied. Forever. Now, he just wants you to come to him as you are. Through Christ, you can have a perfect, intimate, wonderful relationship with God with no fear of judgment or punishment.

It's Not About Your Obedience

Under the Law—the old way of relating to God—it was all about your obedience. But under grace—the new way of relating to God—it's no longer about your obedience. We must come to God based on the obedience of Christ and his perfection, not ours.

We have to stop relying on our own efforts, trying harder, and our vain attempts to please God, and instead trust that Christ has already done everything needed to please God. If we can trust in Christ's obedience and his perfect relationship with the Father, then we can come to God, as we are, broken and in need of his help.

Isn't obedience important? Can we just go out and sin?

The Law of Love far exceeds any law based on rules and regulations. If I were to go to my wife and say, "Honey, the only reason I don't commit adultery is because the Bible says it's wrong," I just might get slapped. The real reason I don't commit adultery is because I love my wife with all of my heart. The Law of Love is far more powerful a deterrent to sin than the law of rules and regulations.

When we live in Christ and trust in his obedience, then God's love grows deeper and deeper into our hearts. And this perfect love of his casts out all fear (1 John 4:18).

Prayer: *Father, help me understand how you fully dealt with sin on the Cross and that you are no longer counting sin against me. Show me how I am free in Christ.*

Finding Spiritual Rest

Over the years, and especially in the past few years, I've experienced a wonderfully deep sense of rest in my soul. It's not so much the rest from being free from anxiety and panic attacks, although that's part of it. It's a deep sense of rest in my relationship with God. That divine rest has been an anchor in my soul for all the other rest.

Hebrews 4:11 says we should diligently work or even "labor" to enter into this rest of God. Sounds a bit like an oxymoron, doesn't it? *Work hard to find rest.*

Here's what I've learned about God's rest: you can't find rest in what you see around you. God's rest is trusting in him no matter what the circumstances are.

God prepared the Promised Land for the children of Israel. As Moses led them through the wilderness, they came to the edge of this new territory. It was time to enter in, so they sent spies to see what was before them.

That was their first mistake. Why didn't they just believe God? Why did they have to see it with their own eyes?

The key to finding rest is **not to** focus on what you **see**, but to focus on what God **says**. The Bible says it this way,

> *Set your mind on things above, not on things on the earth.* (Colossians 3:2)

When you focus on what you see, you will be discouraged. You will not be able to rest in circumstances. You must find rest in "things above."

To take your eyes off of this world effectively, and to "look above," starts with what you believe.

Do you ever wonder...

- *Does God hear my prayers?*
- *Has God abandoned me?*
- *Have I sinned so badly that God won't answer my prayers?*
- *Maybe I've committed the unpardonable sin.*
- *I sinned too much, and I can't be forgiven.*

These are all lies!

- In Christ... God hears your prayers.
- In Christ... God has not abandoned you.
- In Christ... All of your sin—ALL OF IT—has been taken away.
- If you're worried that you've committed the unpardonable sin, then you haven't.
- Where sin abounds, grace much more abounds.

By his grace, we are saved through faith (Ephesians 2:8). "Through faith." It's all about what we believe. If you can believe that God loves you, wants you, and invites you into his presence as you are, you will find incredible rest!

Prayer: *Father, help me to see all that Christ has done for me so that I can enter into the rest you have prepared for me, not by what I do but by what I believe.*

Finding Hope in the Seasons of Fear

When those dark seasons of fear and panic hit, it can feel very hopeless. You pray, you beg, and you plead with God to take it away, but the fear continues to taunt and terrorize your soul. It can be very discouraging, but I have some encouraging words for you.

Let God Speak to You

> *The Lord says, "I will guide you along the best pathway for your life. I will advise you and watch over you."* (Psalms 32:8)

God desires to speak into your life through his tender, loving, divine whispers. Take some time to learn how to hear God's voice. It may feel foreign to you, but God desires to speak to you. Jesus said, *"My sheep hear my voice"* (John 10:27).

The problem is that we often don't take time to listen. The busyness and distractions of the day make it difficult to be still and tune in our spirits to God's Spirit. Nevertheless, we must listen. *"Faith comes by hearing"* (Romans 10:17), so we must take time to listen so that believing will be easier and easier.

Trust Him

When I look back at my life and think through all those years that I struggled with crippling anxiety, panic attacks, and fear, it all came down to trust. I believed that I was in charge of my own life. I was responsible for my own peace, my own safety, my own future. The weight of my life was on me.

I can tell you from experience that this is not a good way to live. The more I learned to trust God and rest in his love for me, the more peace and rest I experienced. The more I surrendered control to him, the less I had to strive. Today, I'm still learning to trust him more and surrender more.

Here are some areas in which I have learned to trust God more:

- I trust that all of my sins—past, present, and future—are forgiven (1 John 1:9).
- I trust that my eternal destination is heaven (1 John 5:13).
- I trust that God will provide all my needs (Philippians 4:19).
- I trust that God will protect me and keep me safe (Psalm 91).
- I trust that he is always with me, even until the end of the age (Matthew 28:20).

I encourage you to stop believing the lies, let God speak to you, and then trust him. Even when we are faithless, he is faithful (2 Timothy 2:13).

Prayer: *Father, help me break through this hopelessness. Speak to my heart and show me how much you love me.*

Finding Peace Through Transformation

We search, we struggle, and we desperately grasp for whatever peace we can find. For some, temporary peace comes through worldly escapes like food, alcohol, medication, and entertainment. For others, there's no peace at all—just a continual, sleepless torment.

Deep inside each of us, though, is a craving and desire for true peace. We want our bodies and our mind to be at rest, but the battle within just seems to rage on. Where is that peace? How can we find it?

Let me start by sharing three ways we **wrongly** search for peace:

Try Harder

In the "try harder" solution, we carry the burden of finding peace. Results are our responsibility, the fruit of our effort. It's common in our culture to expect results from trying harder. We find it in schools, in our jobs, in almost every area of our lives. "Just try harder, and then you'll succeed."

Here's the problem—it doesn't bring true, complete healing. Sure, some areas of success come through trying harder, but they are often superficial and short-lived. Trying harder puts all of the burden and effort on you.

Trying harder also has the exact opposite effect. The

more strength, effort, and emotional energy you pour into trying harder, the more adrenaline you release and the more anxiety you create. Remember the campfire example: when you try to put it out by blowing on it, you feed it more oxygen, and it burns hotter. The same is true with trying harder—it only feeds the anxiety and adrenaline.

Wait on God

If trying harder is at one end of the self-effort spectrum, then waiting on God is at the other. It's the notion that we can do nothing on our own, so wait on God. Like the "try harder" solution, there are certain elements of truth in this solution. Sure, there are times we need to engage our will, and there are times we need to wait on God. What I'm referring to, however, is that passive "waiting" that does nothing to change.

Yes, there are times we need to wait on God, but it's far more important that we press into God, hear his voice, and respond to him. Simply waiting on God and doing nothing will not bring lasting peace into our lives.

More Information

Another common response is more information. Over the past two decades, access to information has increased tremendously. There are massive amounts of books, teachings, seminars, workshops, how-to's and a litany of informational resources. Again, information is not bad. We are to grow in our understanding and knowledge, but information alone cannot transform us. Knowing the truth in our minds does not make it real in our hearts.

Look at the Pharisees in Jesus' time. They were a wealth of information and knowledge. They knew Scripture inside and out. If information alone could bring healing, then they would have walked in complete freedom. However, they didn't. Knowledge and information did not change their hearts.

So, what is the solution? Is there hope for those struggling to find peace? Yes! There is hope! The key is transformation through revelation.

Transformation

Don't copy the behavior and customs of this world, but let God transform you into a new person by changing the way you think. Then you will learn to know God's will for you, which is good and pleasing and perfect. (Romans 12:2)

The key to finding peace is not trying harder, waiting on God, or learning the right information—the key to finding peace is transformation that comes through believing what God says. Let me explain.

For transformation to take place, we must surrender to God's way of doing things instead of trying to make it happen on our own. God created each of us to be transformed into the image of his son (Romans 8:29). When we were saved, we were given a new heart (Ezekiel 11:19) and we are now a new creation (2 Corinthians 5:17). We are transformed when we believe the truth of what God says about us.

"Without faith, it's impossible to please God." (Hebrews 11:6)

God is not pleased with our own strength and effort to find peace. God is pleased when we believe what he says about us.

I encourage you to take time to listen to God's voice. Let him speak his transforming love over you. God is at work in you, and he desires for you to live a life full of peace. If you're not sure how to hear God, go back and read the chapter on Hearing God's Voice.

Prayer: *Father, open up my spiritual eyes to your transformation process. Help me surrender to the healing work of Christ in my life.*

Why Should God Answer My Prayers?

Have you ever felt like your prayers are not being heard? You pray for peace, healing, or financial provision, but it seems like nothing happens. You press in deep with fasting, dedication, and devotion, but still, the response is painful silence. You start to question, "Why should God answer my prayers?"

That's actually a good question. Why should God answer your prayers?

Think about it for a moment. Stop reading this message, get a piece of paper, and write down why you think God should answer your prayers.

Do any of these sound familiar?

- *I prayed for a long time.*
- *I fasted when I prayed.*
- *I have been very devoted this week.*
- *I really meant it when I prayed.*
- *I repented of all my sins.*
- *I ended my prayer with "in Jesus' name."*
- *I've done many good things this week.*

While these sound good and important on the surface, these are not reasons why God should answer our prayers.

Prayers Don't Move God

That sounds wrong, doesn't it? We've been taught to press in, intercede, and "move heaven" with our prayers, but I don't believe it's scriptural. I don't believe we can "move God with our prayers," because God already moved on our behalf two thousand years ago when Jesus died on the Cross. Everything that we can ask for today was provided through Christ: salvation, healing (physical and emotional), freedom, provision, and deliverance.

> Blessed be the God and Father of our Lord Jesus Christ, who **has blessed us** with every spiritual blessing in the heavenly places in Christ.
> (Ephesians 1:3, emphasis mine)

We should pray that God would open our eyes and renew our minds to see what we already have in Christ. Notice this scripture states "has blessed us"—it is past tense. It has already been done!

You Will Never Be Good Enough

Often when we pray, we feel like our prayers are heard more when we're doing good and less when we're doing bad. When we sin, we rarely go to God in prayer, thinking that our mistakes will hinder our prayers. We believe that our good works please God and that our sin displeases God.

There's only one thing that pleases God: faith. Believing

pleases God.

> *Without faith (believing) it is impossible to please him.* (Hebrews 11:6a)

So, what do we need to believe? We must believe that...

Only Christ Is Good Enough

No matter how hard we try, we cannot be good enough.

> *There is no one who does good, there is not even one.* (Romans 3:12b)

That is why God sent his Son into the earth. Jesus was the perfect, sinless sacrifice (Hebrews 7:26). Through his life on earth, he fulfilled all requirements of the Law (Romans 8:3-4). Only Christ is good enough.

In Christ, God Hears Our Prayers

When we receive Christ into our hearts, we immediately receive his righteousness, his goodness. God takes our sin and replaces it with the righteousness of Christ. Here's how Scripture describes it:

> *For [God] made [Jesus] who knew no sin to be sin for us, that we might become the righteousness of God in Him.* (2 Corinthians 5:21)

In Christ, God only sees our goodness. That is why we should pray for God to renew our minds and transform us from the inside out (identity), not from the outside in (actions).

For God to hear and answer your prayers, remember these two things:

- Put your faith in Christ. Start by making that heavenly exchange (replacing your sin with Christ's righteousness).
- When you pray, do not trust in your ability to do good. Trust only in Christ's goodness.

In my own life, I have seen an incredible transformation from fear to peace. It did not come through great Bible studies, long periods of fasting, or doing good in my life. It came from putting all my faith and trust in the goodness of Christ.

Prayer: *Father, open my eyes to this truth that answered prayer comes through the goodness of Christ. Help me see that I am righteous in Christ.*

What Does God Think of Me?

Have you ever asked yourself that question? Maybe not out loud, but in your heart?

I think it's a great question, and we should ask ourselves what God thinks about us. Sadly, though, I think that we often "hear" the wrong response. What we "hear," typically, is the result of years of faulty thinking patterns, bad programming, and a worldly upbringing.

Once you grasp the truth of what God thinks about you and how much he loves you, it will set you free!

> *You shall know the truth and the truth shall make you free.* (John 8:32)

When you understand the depths of God's love for you, his *"perfect love will cast out all fear"* (1 John 4:18). However, you have to be transformed by renewing your mind (Romans 12:2). You have to change the way you think, and when you do, fear and panic will have no hold on you.

Righteousness

How do you define your righteousness—your right-standing with God? Is God pleased with you or is he mad at you? Are you only righteous when you haven't sinned or after you've done a bunch of good things?

Too often, we define our righteousness by our actions

or thoughts: "When I sin, I am not righteous, but when I confess my sins, pray, read the Bible, and do good things, then I'm righteous again. Then, God accepts me."

But, that's **not** how the Bible defines righteousness. Under the New Covenant, there was a great exchange. Jesus, who was perfect and righteous before God, became sin for us so that we could become righteous before our Father.

> *For God made Christ who knew no sin to be sin for us, that we might become the righteousness of God in Him.* (2 Corinthians 5:21)

Jesus became sin and we became righteous. There's nothing we can do to become righteous. We simply have to believe in the great exchange and put our faith in Christ. He is our righteousness. He makes us perfect and pleasing to God. *"Christ's one act of righteousness makes all people right in God's sight and gives them life"* (Romans 5:18).

Sin

What about when I sin? Do I lose my righteousness? Do I lose my right standing with God?

This is where I believe most of our upbringing and worldly programming works against us. Do well in school, and get good grades. Do well on your job, and get a promotion. So, naturally, when we think about

God's view of us, we filter it through this clouded, broken-hearted lens and fall short. When compared to God's holiness, we will always fall short. Always.

That's why it's absolutely essential we let God transform our hearts and change the way we think about our standing with him. As long as we live with this wrong understanding that God is only pleased with our performance, then we'll never be able to receive all of God's love for us. Your sins are forgiven. Your past sins, your present sins, and your future sins are forgiven in Christ. *"He has removed our sins as far from us as the East is from the West"* (Psalms 103:12).

There's only one thing standing between you and God—what you believe about your righteousness. If you believe you are sinful and that God rejects you, then you will pull away and not come to God when you need him most. However, if you believe that Christ has cleansed you from all unrighteousness (1 John 1:9), then you can boldly come to the throne of grace in your time of need (Hebrews 4:16), not based on your performance but on the performance of Christ.

I encourage you to learn more about your right-standing with God. The more you understand and believe that you are perfect in God's eyes in Christ, the more you will open your heart to his fear-breaking, anxiety-conquering love.

Don't ask yourself, "Is God pleased with me?" Ask yourself, "Is God pleased with Christ?" Because when you put your faith in Christ, you become the righteousness of God. You are perfectly pleasing to God!

Prayer: *Father, open my eyes and my heart to truly believe I am perfect in your sight through Christ.*

Is Freedom Possible?

Through most of my early life, when fear and panic attacks were rampant, I would often ask myself this question: can I really be free from this?

I believed that maybe I would have this condition for the rest of my life. Or I would have to take medication every day for the rest of my life. There was even a time I thought God was telling me I would have panic attacks until the day I died.

Today, I believe something much different. I now believe with all of my heart that freedom is possible for everyone. God does not favor one person over another (Acts 10:34), and Jesus died so that we can all be *"blessed with every spiritual blessing in heaven"* (Ephesians 1:3).

I no longer battle with panic attacks. I also no longer take medication for anxiety and panic attacks.

I remember the day when hope came alive in me, that freedom was truly possible. I was sitting in a counseling office. Again. *What questions will this guy ask?* I no longer had to rehearse my answers. I had talked about my "condition" so many times before.

But this time was different. Instead of asking me questions, he told him his story about panic attacks. Immediately, he had my attention. He shared how it crippled him for years, how it caused his world to shrink, and how he had no hope for so long. But then, he shared how he was now completely free. No more panic attacks. I was really listening!

That day sparked a new hope in me. It started me on a journey to freedom. I believed I could be free from this crippling condition.

Today, I shout it from the rooftops: FREEDOM IS POSSIBLE!

With God, All Things Are Possible

> *Is anything too hard for the Lord?* (Genesis 18:14)

> *Jesus said, "What is impossible for people is possible with God."* (Luke 18:27)

I now believe that it is possible to be completely free from anxiety, fear and panic attacks. Nothing is too hard for God. He is able to set you free. I really believe that because I have seen it in my own life, and in the lives of many others.

Prayer: *Father, I may have been hopeless for a long time, but today, let your hope come alive in me. Show me that I can experience freedom from fear, anxiety, and panic attacks.*

The Faith for Freedom

How many times have you said to yourself: *I wish I had more faith? If I had more faith, I know I could overcome these fears and panic attacks.*

I said that for years! *Lord, give me more faith. Help my unbelief. Lord, give me a mustard seed of faith.* But nothing really changed in me. My situation stayed the same. I started to wonder if my prayers for more faith were accurate. After some deep study of the Bible in this area of faith, I started to change the way I prayed, because my understanding of faith was not accurate.

Here's what I learned about faith:

What is Faith?

Remember when we looked at the Greek? The two Greek words that appear throughout the New Testament are "*pistis*" (noun) and "*pisteuo*" (verb). Interestingly, most Bibles translate the noun as "faith" and the verb as "believe," but these two words mean the same thing.

Too often, we define faith as something different from belief. We talk about the Baptist faith or getting more faith, but I don't think that's biblically accurate. Faith simply means belief. When you say, "I wish I had more faith," you can also say, "I wish I believed more."

Faith Does Not Move God

This may sound weird, even heretical, but it's one of the most powerful truths I've learned.

Faith is simply renewing our minds to receive what is already ours. That's why Romans 12:1-2 encourages us to be transformed by the renewing of the mind. We need to think differently.

When Paul prayed for the Ephesians, he asked God to give them a spirit of wisdom and revelation in the knowledge of Him, that the eyes of their understanding would be enlightened (Ephesians 1:17-21).

We have available to us today this incredible spiritual inheritance, and we must pray that the eyes of our understanding would be enlightened so we can see what we already have in Christ.

Misdirected Faith

Too often, we focus our faith on things. We ask God for peace, healing, strength, and provision. I have done this quite a bit myself. Sometimes those prayers are answered, but I don't believe this is where we should focus our faith.

When we focus our faith on things, we can easily miss the Source of those things. What you focus on will organize your life. If you focus on freedom, healing, and peace, then those things will organize your life, and you will be consumed with finding things instead of finding God. Jesus said, "**Seek first** the kingdom of God and His righteousness, and all these things shall be added to you" (Matthew 6:33, emphasis mine).

Our faith—what we believe—should be focused on knowing Christ and his righteousness. Jesus is the Author and Finisher of our faith (Hebrews 12:2). He should be our complete focus.

In John 6:28-29, the disciples came to Jesus and asked him, "What does God want us to do?" They were asking Jesus where they should focus their faith. Jesus responded, *"This is what God wants you to do: Believe in the One he has sent."*

I want to encourage you to focus your faith on Christ. Seek first his righteousness, and all the things you need—freedom, joy, rest, healing, and peace—will begin working in your life. Renew your mind through prayer, scripture, and Bible study. Ask the Holy Spirit to guide you and teach you all things.

Prayer: *Father, help me refocus my faith on your Son, Jesus, the Author and Finisher of my faith.*

Sinner or Saint

The more I learn about who we are in Christ, the more I realize this incredible truth: sin has no power over us. You are no longer a sinner. Do you find that hard to believe? Let me explain.

In Christ, we are dead to sin (Romans 6:2). We are free from sin (Romans 6:18-22). It was dealt with on the Cross. When we receive Christ and are baptized into his death, we have died to sin. We are no longer "sinners." Rather, we are "saints" (called ones).

In Christ, you are not a sinner. You are a saint, and you can boldly go to the throne of grace in your time of need (Hebrews 4:16). Not only that, you are seated with Christ in heavenly places (Ephesians 2:6). Moreover, if God cannot sit in the presence of sin, then you must be completely free from sin.

Think about this Scripture where Jesus explains why it is good for him to go to heaven and send us the Holy Spirit. He explains what the Holy Spirit's job is here on earth.

And when he [the Holy Spirit] has come, he will convict the world of sin, and of righteousness, and of judgment:

of sin, because they do not believe in Me;

of righteousness, because I go to My Father and you see Me no more;

of judgment, because the ruler of this world is judged. (John 16:8-11)

It tells us immediately what the conviction of sin is, "because they do not believe in [Christ]." Notice it didn't say, "of sin, because they do not know the difference between right and wrong." According to this Scripture, sin is not believing in Christ.

What most believers don't understand is that if you have put your faith in Christ, then you are righteous.

For by grace you have been saved through faith, and that not of yourselves; it is the gift of God, not of works, lest anyone should boast. (Ephesians 2:8-9)

The Holy Spirit's job is to convict Christians that they are righteous in Christ. In addition, through that righteousness, we have access to God our Father. We are children of God (John 1:12). We are justified (Romans 5:1). We are friends of Christ (John 15:15). We are saints (Ephesians 1:1).

Can Christians still commit sin? Yes, of course. However, according to Romans 7, it's the sin in my flesh, not who I am in Christ.

For what I am doing, I do not understand. For what I will to do, that I do not practice; but what I hate, that I do. If, then, I do what I will not to do, I agree with the law that it is good. But now, it is no longer I who do it, but sin that dwells in me. (Romans 7:15-17)

Paul talked about this "body of death." He said in the next verse (18), *"I know that in me (that is, in my flesh) nothing good dwells."* He understood that in the flesh there may be sin, but it doesn't define who we are.

In Christ, we are saints, we are free, and we are seated with him at the right hand of God.

Prayer: *Father, help me see that in Christ I am a saint. I am not a sinner. You have cleansed me from all sin. Help me understand that I am righteous because of what Christ did for me.*

Real Repentance

After a deeper study of repentance in the original language, I think we've got it wrong.

Read these two verses from a modern Bible translation:

> Peter's words pierced their hearts, and they said to him and to the other apostles, "Brothers, what should we do?" Peter replied, "Each of you must **repent of your sins** and turn to God, and be baptized in the name of Jesus Christ for the forgiveness of your sins. Then you will receive the gift of the Holy Spirit." (Acts 2:37-38, emphasis mine)

> Now **repent of your sins** and turn to God, so that your sins may be wiped away. (Acts 3:19, emphasis mine)

You hear this term quite often, "Repent of your sins," implying that repentance of sins is a turning away from sins, to stop sinning. I don't think that's what the original language was implying. If you search through a more accurate word-for-word translation (KJV or NKJV), you can't find a single instance of Jesus saying, "Repent of your sins." He never said that. He did say, "Repent, for the Kingdom of God is at hand."

Look at the original Greek for "repent"— *metanoeo*. It comes from two words, "*meta*" and "*noeo*".

"*Meta*" means an over-arching change. There's a difference between morphing and meta-morphing. Morphing is changing from within something similar. Meta-morphing, on the other hand, is changing from a caterpillar to a butterfly. It's an over-arching change—a broader, higher-level change.

"*Noeo*" is where we get the word knowledge. It means to think, to perceive, to understand.

So, combine the two "*meta-noeo*," and you have a word that means "an over-arching change in how you understand or perceive."

The message Jesus had for us was not "stop sinning so that you change your thinking"—his message was "change the way you think, and you'll stop sinning."

Jesus died *"once for all"* (Hebrews 10:10) and provided *"eternal redemption"* (Hebrews 9:12). He no longer has to die for your sins. All your sins (past, present, and future) were taken care of once and for all.

Now that our sins are gone, we need to repent.

Prayer: *Father, help me realize that all of my sins are gone, dealt with, cleansed. In Christ, I am fully and completely accepted by you. Teach me how to change my worldly perspective to a Kingdom perspective. Teach me to see you more clearly.*

Financial Anxiety

When you think of money or finances, is your stomach in knots? Does tax season stress you out? Are you living paycheck to paycheck? Are you constantly fretting layoffs or "restructuring"?

Finances can be a very anxious experience for many, even those who are well off. Managing money can be stressful. Married couples often cite finances as the leading cause of conflict in marriage. It's an incredibly serious issue in people's lives.

Can you find peace in stressful financial situations? Can finances really become a place of peace and rest, or must they always be feared and anxiety-provoking?

When it comes to our financial economy, I'm terribly concerned for our country. Consumer debt is at an all-time high. Credit companies have made it so easy to "buy now and pay later." For one small monthly fee, you can have whatever you want. How many of those "small monthly fees" do you have?

This credit-driven lifestyle has made it too easy to spend more than we make. I recently heard a statistic on consumer spending in America. Through most of the 1900s, people spent on average about 30% less than what they made. That means people were saving money. Today, the average American spends more than they earn. That means nothing is being saved. Nothing is put away for unforeseen circumstances.

I can see why financial anxiety is rampant these days. The loss of a job, an emergency house repair, the car breaks down—all of this can be terribly stressful when it comes to finances.

So, is there hope? Can you be free from financial anxiety? I shout a hearty YES. You can be free. However, it may take time and serious discipline. It probably took you years to get where you are now. For many, it'll take years to dig out of the financial pit. Here's the beautiful thing—God is faithful and he cares for you, even your finances. And he wants to help.

Today, my wife and I live in financial freedom. Moreover, it's not because we have lots of money. In fact, I'm a freelancer and so our finances ebb and flow depending on projects. Our financial freedom is a result of clear money management skills, and the discipline to live by those skills.

We live on a budget. We no longer use credit cards. We only buy used cars, and at the end of each month, we have money left over. Amazingly, we don't feel at all constricted by this lifestyle. Quite the opposite—this lifestyle has given us incredible freedom.

"But you don't know where we are. We've maxed out our credit cards. My husband lost his job. These medical bills keep getting higher and higher. We can barely get by."

Here's the most important message I learned about finances: it's not a matter of how much or how little you make; it's a matter of your heart. Financial freedom starts in your heart. Listen to what Jesus said,

> Wherever your treasure is, there your heart and thoughts will also be. (Matthew 6:21)

Where is your treasure? A new car, a big house, a styling pair of jeans? Or is your treasure in your family, your peace, or God? You see, where you put your money is where your heart is. Your money always follows your heart. So make sure your heart is right when it comes to finances.

When my wife and I first got married, we were in debt. I was into new cars, new stereo equipment, and new things. Therefore, when I prayed for financial freedom, I expected God to deposit a big sum of money into my account. What he did, though, was deposit wisdom into my heart. True financial freedom starts in your heart.

If you're struggling with finances, I want to encourage you that you can be free from financial anxiety. God desires to help you, first with your heart and then with your finances. I have seen God move in amazing ways when it comes to finances, both in my life and in the lives of those we have counseled. There are great resources to help you in this journey towards financial freedom like Dave Ramsey (http://daveramsey.com) or Crown Financial (http://www.crown.org/).

Prayer: *Father, I need your help with finances. Financial anxiety is consuming me. I've made some bad money decisions in the past, and the financial consequences are overwhelming. First, change my heart. Then, give me a strategy to get my finances under control. Help me start down the road to financial freedom.*

The Power Within

By the time 1991 rolled around, I had struggled with anxiety and panic attacks most of my life. Yet 1991 was a pivotal year for me. That's the year I put my faith in Christ. I was 26 years old.

When I became a Christian, I expected the fear and panic to instantly go away. I expected those daily battles with anxiety and panic to stop. But they didn't. My logical mind really struggled with this. After all, didn't Jesus defeat death on the Cross? If so, then surely anxiety and panic were easy for him. Right?

Yet I prayed. I begged. I pleaded with God to free me from the fear. Nothing happened. God was not moving on my behalf.

Or, so I thought.

Turns out, God already moved on my behalf. God already defeated fear and panic on the Cross two thousand years ago. You see, I was waiting on God, but the whole time, he was waiting on me.

Let me share a Scripture with you. It starts out like this:

> *Now to Him (God) who is able to do exceedingly abundantly above all that we ask or think...*
> (Ephesians 3:20a)

Sounds amazing, doesn't it?

Here's what God is able to do:

- Exceedingly.
- Abundantly.
- Above all.
- We can ask or think.

God can do a lot in our lives; yet, there is one thing that can limit him. There is actually something that can limit the work of God in our lives. That something is described in the second half of that scripture that we often leave off: "God is able to do exceedingly abundantly above all that we ask or think **according to the power that works in us.**"

The word according here means "to the limit of." God can do amazing, wonderful, powerful things in us, but we can limit God with our thoughts, our unbelief, and our choices.

When it comes to panic and anxiety, we can't wait on God to answer our prayers. You see, he's already answered them. Through Christ, we have the power in us to stand against fear. We have the authority to resist the enemy. We have everything we need for victory.

It took me a few years to grasp this truth after becoming a Christian, but once I did, fear lost its power in my life. Fear no longer told me how to live. Fear lost its grip in my life, because the power of Christ was already inside of me, and if Christ lives in your heart, then you too have the power of Christ in you.

Let me share a recent example of how this works. Years ago, when fear reigned in my heart, I was terrified of driving. I hated driving long distances, and I hated going to places I had never been. Panic would sweep over me as I drove. Often, I would give into the fear, and it would consume my body and mind. Total panic.

When I realized that I had the power of Christ in me, I decided no longer to obey those fearful thoughts. Sure, they still came, but I wouldn't give in to them. Fear would say, "Don't go there. Don't drive. Don't leave your house. Don't go this way." Nevertheless, today, when I hear those thoughts, I make it a priority to do those things that irrational fear tells me to avoid.

In the summer of 2006, my wife was finishing up her one-month stay in Mexico. She had flown down Guanajuato, Mexico, to study Spanish. She was scheduled to fly home on the weekend, but my son and I decided to drive down into deep Mexico and surprise her. Now, fear was saying, "That's stupid. You could get lost or hurt or worse." In addition, others around me spoke similar words of fear. The more fear spoke, the more determined I was to go.

My son I and made the seventeen hour drive into Guanajuato, Mexico, and surprised my wife. Then we drove eighteen hours back. It was a wonderful trip! We had the best time. My wife was so surprised, and this is now one of our most cherished memories. The drive was amazing, peaceful, and beautiful. There was no fear.

If I had listened to fear, we would have never had such a wonderful experience.

My son and I documented our entire trip on video. So, if you would like to share in our journey, check out this link: http://j.mp/SoG-RoadTrip

Prayer: *Father, show me where I have limited you. Teach me to release your power through me so that you can do exceedingly, abundantly above all I can ask or think, in the name of Jesus.*

ABOUT THE AUTHOR

Russ Pond started sharing his journey with fear and panic attacks online at his website, *Season of Peace* (http://season.org) in 1995. Over the years, hundreds of thousands of people have visited the website and continue to learn more about God's desire to set them free from fear and panic attacks. This is Russ' second book based on the writings from his blog.

You can follow the *Season of Peace* ministry at:
- http://season.org
- http://facebook.com/SeasonofPeace
- http://twitter.com/SeasonofPeace

Russ and his wife, Angela, celebrated 20 years of marriage this year (2013). Their son, Caleb, started college at the University of Texas at Dallas in Game Design & Development.

Russ continues to run his video production business in the Dallas area. He has also produced three feature films, and is now starting work on this next one.

You can follow Russ online at:
- http://facebook.com/russpond
- http://twitter.com/russpond
- http://toppup.com
- http://russpond.com
- http://about.me/russpond

REFERENCES

King James Version (KJV) – by Public Domain.

New King James Version (NKJV) The Holy Bible, Copyright © 1982 by Thomas Nelson, Inc.

New International Version® (NIV®) Copyright © 1973, 1978, 1984, 2011 by Biblica, Inc.® Used by permission.

New American Standard Bible (NASB) Copyright © 1960, 1962, 1963, 1968, 1971, 1972, 1973, 1975, 1977, 1995 by The Lockman Foundation.

English Standard Version (ESV) Copyright © 2001 by Crossway Bibles, a division of Good News Publishers.

Amplified Bible (AMP) Copyright © 1954, 1958, 1962, 1964, 1965, 1987 by The Lockman Foundation.

New Living Translation (NLT) Copyright © 1996, 2004, 2007 by Tyndale House Publishers, Inc.

Endnotes

[i] Bob Hamp, http://bobhamp.com/freedom/its-time/ (2009).

[ii] Bob Hamp, *Think Differently, Live Differently* (2010), 32-33.

[iii] Hamp, 60.

[iv] Mick Mooney, *Look! The finished work of Jesus: A Message Of God's Radical Love For You* (2010), Kindle Locations 643-644, Lightview Media.

[v] Alan Smith, http://alansmithonline.com/ (2007).

[vi] *New Oxford American Dictionary* (2005).

[vii] Cornel Marais, *So You Think Your Mind Is Renewed?* (2009), Kindle Locations 113-115, New Nature Publications.

[viii] Hamp, 71-73.

[ix] From the International Bible Study, 1984

[x] Paul Ellis, *The Gospel in Ten Words* (2012), Kindle Locations 806-807, KingsPress.

[xi] Joseph Prince, *God's Glory Has Been Restored To You* (2010)

[xii] Pierre Teilhard de Chardin

[xiii] Greg Boyd, http://reknew.org

[xiv] John Trench, *Synonyms of the New Testament*

[xv] Gregory Boyd and Al Larson, *Escaping the Matrix: Setting Your Mind Free to Experience Real Life in Christ* (2005), 34.

[xvi] Dykstra, Eric, *Grace On Tap* (2013), Kindle Locations 2102-2103, Crossing Church Publishing.

[xvii] Phil Drysdale, http://phildrysdale.com/2011/04/why-do-i-sin/ (2011).

Made in the USA
San Bernardino, CA
02 September 2014